THROUGH THE VALLEY
SHADOW

Thanks
Rod *[signature]*

Thank you
Misty Corkovell

OF THE

DEDICATION

Victims of crime are often forgotten, with their plights over-shadowed by other issues. For the crimes detailed in this book, there were many victims. Two teenage girls, Tanya Smith and Misty Cockerill, were viciously attacked by an opportunistic sexual predator. The family of Tanya Smith, while grieving the loss of their child, were forced to endure the killer's continued insults and theft of their daughter's gravestone. The family of Misty Cockerill lived in the isolation of witness protection for seven months, knowing the killer's ongoing threats against Misty, who had barely survived his first attack. There were also three Abbotsford women who the killer claimed as his conquests. And finally, the residents of Abbotsford, Chilliwack, and other Fraser Valley communities who lived in fear, knowing that a sexual predator and murderer was at large and threatening to kill again.

On behalf of the police officers who worked on this investigation, this book is dedicated to the victims of crime. In particular to the memory of Tanya Smith, whose young life was senselessly taken, and to the courage of her friend Misty Cockerill, who fought back against incredible injuries to survive and help the police and prosecutors to capture and convict the killer.

Murder victim, Tanya Smith

Surviving victim, Misty Cockerill

TABLE OF CONTENTS

FOREWORD

Anyone familiar with the case of the Abbotsford Killer will
no doubt recall it as one of the strangest and most frightening murder cases imaginable. You had to live here in the
City of Abbotsford to fully appreciate just how frightening
it was, but suffice it to say, no case before or after this murder caused so many women to be so noticeably afraid for
their personal safety. And for good reason; over the course of
nearly seven months after phoning Abbotsford Police to brag
that he was the man responsible for the brutal sexual attack
on two innocent teenage girls walking home one night, the
Abbotsford Killer boasted that they would never catch him,
and he would do it again. One of the two girls was murdered
in the attack, and it is nothing short of a miracle that the
other managed to survive. The case was particularly strange
because the killer acted brazenly as he taunted the police.

As strange as the case was, at the end of the day there proved
to be nothing special about the killer himself. All indications
were that he was nothing more than your run-of-the-mill
sexual psychopath, a textbook example of a serial killer caught
early, and a man who was so full of himself, it was essentially his

own ego that led to his arrest. He thought he was smarter than the police, but as it turned out, he wasn't even close.

While the Abbotsford Killer could be described as a typical sexual psychopath, he is, nonetheless, of particular interest to those of us who study criminals, because while there aren't many sexual psychopaths out there, as criminals go, few are as dangerous or as difficult to catch. Every known case becomes important to refining our understanding of what makes these people tick and what behavior patterns can be expected of them. And for that reason alone, this book makes an important contribution to the library of information on sexual psychopaths who kill.

Perhaps what is more significant about this book is what it tells us about conducting a brilliant police investigation. Most of us never really get a chance to see what goes on in a murder investigation from beginning to end. Here, we do, and in the course of that, we get to see just how thoughtful police were in this case, gathering evidence in a way that would ensure that the killer, once identified, would not escape justice in a criminal trial. In this regard, the book is very unique and, for yet another reason, a "must read."

Darryl Plecas, Ed.D.
RCMP Research Chair
School of Criminology and Criminal Justice
University College of the Fraser Valley

PROLOGUE

The man was standing in front of them almost before they had a chance to comprehend that he had been hidden by the hedge of twelve-foot cedar shrubs paralleling the sidewalk. Holding a baseball bat in one hand, and with a wild look in his eyes, he said, "Do you b***** want to party?" and without awaiting a reply, he walked to them, his arms spread, and pushed them through the cedar shrubs that had hidden him from their approaching view.

Once on the other side of the hedge, the girls found themselves on a small eight-foot-by-eight-foot grassy area in the corner of the cedar hedgerow. This hedgerow was the back boundary of the rear parking lot for the MSA Hospital's Extended Care Unit. Abandoned at this time of night, except for the vehicles of some on-duty staff, the parking area was still in open view and very well lit by parking lot lamps.

Wielding his bat over his head, making his intent to strike apparent, he ordered the girls to take off their clothes. In terror Tanya complied and stripped off her shirt and pants. Seeing that he seemed satisfied with one compliant victim, Misty did not remove any clothing. She stood staring in horror, realizing what was about to happen. The man pushed Tanya to the ground and dropped down behind her on his knees to proceed with his acts of sexual assault. Misty tried coughing and fell to her knees, faking an asthma attack. The attacker responded, his tone annoyed and taunting, "You are faking. If you really had asthma, you would have a puffer with you."

As he started his assault on Tanya, he had to put down the baseball bat to unfasten his own pants. At this point, Misty could have run away to save herself. The rapist was on his knees, his pants down, and she could have gotten away. But she didn't.

INTRODUCTION

Feeling safe from violent crime is something most people seek when choosing a place to live and raise a family. Some say this feeling of security is an illusion, and the potential for violent crime exists around us constantly. Others argue that we are generally safe, and the violent criminals who threaten our safety are the exception rather than the rule.

For seven months between October 1995 and May of 1996, residents in the City of Abbotsford and others throughout the Fraser Valley of British Columbia were forced to live in fear of violent crime. A sexual predator was at large. He had killed once and was threatening to kill again. In cases like this, the entire community is victimized. For many who lived through these events, things would never be the same.

Thankfully, it is not often that communities are faced with this type of killer. This type of criminal is an anomaly. We know from historical crime data that the majority of murders are committed by a person known to the victim. Husbands, wives, neighbors, friends, enemies, lovers, business partners, and many others could fit into this category. Often characterized as "crimes of passion," these murders are

usually committed in circumstances influenced by height-
ened emotions, intoxicants, or both.

Second to these "crimes of passion," a significant and
growing number of murders are committed as retribution to
settle a score or to induce a power threat as seen in gang
murders and contract killings.

The most rare and infrequent type of murder is the
stranger-to-stranger homicide. Some of these murders are
committed incidental to another crime, such as robbery or
breaking and entering. These often happen in circumstances
where the primary crime goes wrong and murder is committed to aid in escape or to eliminate witnesses.

Finally, in the stranger-to-stranger category is the rarest
type of murder, the sexual-predator homicide. These murders
are committed by individuals who live by no rules. Their personal needs, desires, and fantasies are fulfilled through violent
acts of power and control over their victims. Their ultimate
demonstration of power is the taking of their victim's life.

With these killers, psychologists often point out that the
apparent sexual nature of the crime is more about gratification through power and control than the sexual act itself.
Driven to satisfy their needs and unrestricted by conscience
or remorse, these individuals often go on to become serial
killers. These killers are the devious predators. Strangers not
otherwise associated to their victims, they are difficult to
identify and elusive to capture.

When the faceless specter of this kind of killer became a
reality for the small city of Abbotsford British Columbia, the
threat and the fear spread throughout the neighboring Fraser
Valley communities. To capture the Abbotsford Killer, police

agencies from across British Columbia came together to confront their common threat. This is the story of that investigation. For the police, it was like chasing a shadow; for the communities involved, this was truly the shadow of death.

A NICE PLACE TO LIVE

Sitting down to write the story of these events from over a decade ago, it still seems like just yesterday. I don't believe that any police officer who worked on this case will ever forget it. Certainly no one who lived in Abbotsford through this time will.

In October of 1995, the City of Abbotsford had already been my home and workplace for fourteen years. Actually, the community that I had moved to in 1981 was a municipality called Matsqui, and the name had only recently changed to Abbotsford following an amalgamation of the two municipalities.

At the time of their inception, Matsqui was the larger of the two municipalities. Matsqui and Abbotsford had been incorporated in 1892 and 1894 respectively as communities projecting settlement forty miles east into the Fraser Valley from the City of Vancouver. Abbotsford was named by the founding fathers in honor of Harry Abbot, who happened to be the western superintendent for the Canadian Pacific Railway. Reciprocating, the CPR would eventually make Abbotsford Village a scheduled stop on their main line.

Speaking now in terms of very recent history, both areas had only jointly come to be named Abbotsford on January 1, 1995. This joining was all part of a regional amalgamation plan designed to integrate municipal services and save tax dollars.

Prior to this amalgamation, the two distinct municipalities, Matsqui and Abbotsford, had their own municipal infrastructures, including different police departments. The Matsqui Police Department had been established in 1954. The community wanted more police officers, and this required a change from the Royal Canadian Mounted Police RCMP contract in place at the time. Abbotsford was then an RCMP Detachment. It had always been either Provincial Police or RCMP Detachment, as the Provincial contacts had changed over the years. A referendum was held to determine which department would police the two communities. The communities voted to continue with the Matsqui Municipal Police Department that would be renamed to become the Abbotsford Police. The new police department would grow immediately to one hundred officers. RCMP members from the closing Abbotsford Detachment were offered lateral moves into the new department at their current rank and seniority. Only four of the thirty police officers elected to make the move, and the rest took transfers to other RCMP Detachments. The new joined municipality would cover 135 square miles in area, with a population of 110,000 residents.

Historically, the areas Matsqui and Abbotsford had grown and prospered under the watchful eye of the Dutch, Mennonite, and East Indian farmers who had taken advantage of the rich farmlands to develop large dairy, hog, and chicken farms, along with cash crops of strawberries, raspberries, and blueberries.

With more churches per capita than any other area in the Province, the Christian culture was so strong that Abbotsford and Matsqui were known as the Bible Belt of British Columbia. Almost every denomination of church was represented, including the original Sikh Temple built in the early 1900s, now in the shadow of the new Sikh Temple built in the 1980s on the main road through town. This rich mix of ethnic origins and the related places of worship stood as a testimonial to the established history of a diverse and accepting multicultural community.

Now, in the 1990s, with more affordable housing than many other municipalities in the Fraser Valley, Abbotsford was considered a great place for young families to settle. The same quiet semi-rural lifestyle and amenities that had drawn me to settle here with my family in 1981 were luring other traditional Vancouverites into the Valley. Abbotsford was quickly becoming a bedroom community to the City of Vancouver.

This fast-growing population, along with two federal penitentiaries and the main Provincial highway running through the middle of the area, all created dynamics for change that made policing both interesting and challenging.

Along with the standard robberies, thefts, and burglaries, as a police officer here you could always count on some kind of high-profile murder or sexual assault every couple of years. Just prior to the amalgamation in 1994, Matsqui and Abbotsford had been the target of a serial arsonist who ended up setting dozens of fires before he was captured. These kind of serious crimes really threaten the security of the community. The challenge for police is to achieve closure and restore a sense of safety and order as quickly as possible.

Police officers all know that it is their sworn duty "to protect life and property and keep the peace." Most officers take that duty to heart. It becomes part of their personal values, and that extends to the shared values in the culture of the police department. When bad things happen, these shared values draw police officers together for the common cause. They become deadly serious and willing to go the extra mile, even put themselves in harm's way to catch the criminal or solve a crime. Experience had already shown me that the Abbotsford Police had plenty of dedicated officers who felt this way about their community.

From my perspective, the recent name-change from Matsqui Police to Abbotsford Police wasn't a big deal. Having come from the Royal Canadian Mounted Police in Alberta fourteen years earlier, I made the move to the rural municipal police department known as Matsqui Police.

With ten years of prior service as an RCMP constable in various Alberta Detachments, I enjoyed policing in this kind of community. The culture of both the Abbotsford Police Department and the community appealed to me. The police department had a sense of family and belonging that fit with the values of the community we served.

Now, with fourteen years on the department, I was Staff Sergeant in charge of the Criminal Investigations Branch. In this role I managed the activities of the major crime detectives, drug section, street crime team, and forensic identification unit. Likely the best job anyone could hope for, I was in charge of a group of officers who were dedicated and motivated. The biggest challenge was getting sufficient funds from the budget to do all of the projects we needed to do.

THE PREDATOR LURKS

In October of 1995, the Criminal Investigation Branch of the Abbotsford Police was busy but working comfortably on what could be described as routine investigations. Robberies, break and entries, and sexual assaults presented themselves as our daily priorities, and investigations progressed at an acceptable pace. We had no way of knowing the challenge we would soon face.

On Friday October 13, 1995, we were experiencing a mild, extended summer day. That evening many Abbotsford residents enjoyed the last opportunities for barbeques and other outdoor socializing.

Tanya Smith and Misty Cockerill had accepted an invitation from some new friends and went along to an outdoor party in Surrey. It was supposed to be a sleepover at Misty's house that night. Misty's mother, Janet, was out for the evening with her husband, Marty, which made it pretty easy for the two sixteen-year-olds to avoid the usual boundaries of parental scrutiny and get away with some teenage rites of passage, like drinking beer in the park and staying out past curfew. Any cop can tell you that almost every young person will, somewhere along the line, be found out with friends doing these things that their parents would not agree with.

Usually, these adventures of teenage indulgence happen without detection and without tragic consequences. That would not to be the outcome tonight.

When they were dropped off by their new friends in front of Misty's house, it was only twelve o'clock midnight. Since Janet and Marty were not home yet, the girls decided to walk the five blocks to another friend's house, where they believed a birthday party was still in progress. After a quick stop at home, where Misty loaned Tanya a different pair of shoes, the two friends were off again.

The part of Abbotsford City where Misty lived with her mother, Janet, sister, Mandy, and new stepfather, Marty, was a middle-class subdivision on one of the city's main through roads. It was close to the high school that both girls attended, and the area was well known to them. The route they walked was north along Ware Street, then turned right to walk east on Bevan Avenue, bordering the high school property. This led to the back area of the local Matsqui, Sumas, Abbotsford (MSA) Hospital and Extended Care Unit.

As the two friends walked along the well-lit streets, they had no apprehension of danger. After all, they had walked these streets many times before, day and night. Tonight was particularly warm. On their way to the party, they talked about the new friends they had been with that evening and old friends they were about to join at the birthday party. They even joked about the fact that tonight was Friday the thirteenth and laughed that they should be afraid that they might meet a crazed killer.

The man was standing in front of them almost before they had a chance to comprehend that he had been hidden by the hedge of twelve-foot cedar shrubs paralleling the sidewalk. Holding a baseball bat in one hand, and with a wild look in his eyes, he said, "Do you b****** want to party?" and without awaiting a reply, he walked to them, his arms spread, and pushed them through the cedar shrubs that had hidden him from their approaching view.

Once on the other side of the hedge, the girls found themselves on a small eight-foot-by-eight-foot grassy area in the corner of the cedar hedgerow. This hedgerow was the back boundary of the rear parking lot for the MSA Hospital's Extended Care Unit. Abandoned at this time of night, except for the vehicles of some on-duty staff, the parking area was still in open view and very well lit by parking lot lamps.

Wielding his bat over his head, making his intent to strike apparent, he ordered the girls to take off their clothes. In terror Tanya complied and stripped off her shirt and pants. Seeing that he seemed satisfied with one compliant victim, Misty did not remove any clothing. She stood staring in horror, realizing what was about to happen. The man pushed Tanya to the ground and dropped down behind her on his knees to proceed with his acts of sexual assault. Misty tried coughing and fell to her knees, faking an asthma attack. The attacker responded, his tone annoyed and taunting, "You are faking. If you really had asthma, you would have a puffer with you."

As he started his assault on Tanya, he had to put down the baseball bat to unfasten his own pants. At this point,

Misty could have run away to save herself. The rapist was on his knees, his pants down, and she could have gotten away. But she didn't.

It happened very fast, and later she would recall the lost look of terror in Tanya's large, expressive eyes. Perhaps it was her friend's helplessness that drew her next action. Whatever the motivation, Misty did something unusual for a victim in this type of violent crime. She went on the attack. Grabbing the bat from the ground, she hit their attacker as hard as she could across his shoulder.

Reeling from the strike, the man got up from his knees and was quick enough to deflect the second swing. Misty begged him not to strike, but there was no mercy in the man. From this point on, the story becomes less clear. My telling of these events comes as Misty related them to me well after she had recovered from an attack that should have killed her. What she could remember was a wild-eyed man executing a swift and deliberate attack as she pleaded for her life and tried to deflect the blows. Tanya stood frozen in terror. Misty screamed at Tanya to run and begged the attacker to stop. He swore at her, calling her a b****, and telling her that he was going to kill her. She counted seven strikes of the bat before she lost consciousness.

After being knocked out, Misty recalled waking up next to Tanya on the ground and telling her that they needed to go for help. Their attacker was nowhere to be seen. She then recalled groping her way along a chain-link fence and lying down to rest in a garden. As she relates it, the goal in her mind was to find her way home and get to sleep, but that is not what she did. After some time, Misty got up again, and at 4:30 a.m., she somehow stumbled through the doors of the MSA Hospital Emergency Ward, four hours after the initial attack. Doctors and nurses on duty took immediate action. Misty was suffering from a broken arm and hand, along with severe skull fractures consistent with several direct hits to the head. Her body-core temperature showed that she was extremely hypothermic. The natures of her injuries were critical. Even with immediate medical intervention and surgery, she was in danger of dying.

THE INVESTIGATION BEGINS

Amazingly still conscious in the emergency ward, Misty told the nurses that she and her friend Tanya had been attacked, and that Tanya was still out in the bushes near the school. Hospital staff immediately called the Abbotsford Police Department. With that call began what would become one of the most unusual and intense criminal investigations the Abbotsford Police had ever faced.

My bedside phone rang at 5:30 a.m., and as I glanced at the alarm clock and heard the urgent tone in the duty sergeant's voice, I was already pretty sure this wasn't just a routine call to request a detective team. One teenage girl had stumbled into MSA Emergency Ward badly beaten, and her girlfriend was still missing. There was an unknown male attacker. The time and location of the attack were unclear. By the time the sergeant finished his thumbnail briefing, I was wide-awake. Directions were given to call out two teams of detectives. We would meet at the office shortly.

At the same time we were alerted to the situation at the

Abbotsford Emergency Ward, other events were unfolding twenty kilometers to the east at the Vedder Canal.

The Vedder Canal is an extension of the Chilliwack River that flows to the Fraser River. These waterways form the border between the municipal districts of Chilliwack and Abbotsford. Back in 1924, the Vedder Canal was constructed as part of a dyking system engineered to drain Sumas Lake and reclaim thirty thousand acres of rich agricultural land. The area reclaimed was the fertile farmland now known as the Sumas Prairie. Driving through the Fraser Valley, the large, flat expanse of Sumas Prairie is visible from the east side of Abbotsford City to the west edge of Chilliwack City.

The dykes of the Vedder Canal are twenty feet tall in some places; however, during this part of October, the waters of the river are no threat. They are confined to a shallow gravel riverbed about one hundred yards wide. In many places a person can wade across the river with water at only waist level. In the fall the Vedder River is a popular spot for fishermen taking advantage of the Coho salmon run that comes up the river to spawning grounds on the Chilliwack River.

There are always plenty of dedicated anglers up before dawn or camping overnight on the banks of the Vedder River, making their way to secure the best fishing spot for the first light of day. At this time of year, it is possible to drive down off the dyke and come within a few feet of the riverbank. Because of these typical fishing rituals, no one thinks twice about seeing vehicles driving up on the dykes or coming and going from the river's edge at any time day or night in October.

At eight a.m., as the full effects of daylight came to the

river, two fishing buddies worked their way farther into the river toward the better current. One of them focused on the form of a young girl's nude body floating facedown in a shallow backwater area surrounded by brush on one side. Shocked with their discovery, they immediately obtained a cell phone and called 911.

The part of the Vedder River where the body was found is in the jurisdiction of the Chilliwack RCMP. With this kind of discovery, the RCMP immediately called out a team of investigators to start a homicide investigation.

The team of Abbotsford Police investigators following up on the attack on the two girls had contacted Misty's mother to come to the hospital. Other police officers, including dog handlers, were still searching all of the bush areas near the school in response to Misty's report that Tanya was in the bush. Misty continued in and out of consciousness, and as she did, she provided further information. Some of the information was eventually evaluated to be incoherent. At one point as she drifted in and out, she said the attacker was seven feet tall, he was married to one of the nurses in the emergency ward, his name was Steven Suade, and he worked in a chocolate factory.

Abbotsford investigators worked with Misty's address book and school annual to confirm Tanya's identity. At nine a.m., around the same time information came in that the Chilliwack RCMP were investigating the discovery of a female body in the Vedder Canal, it was confirmed with Misty's mother, Janet, that sixteen-year-old Tanya Smith was the girl we were looking for.

Abbotsford detectives attended at the Vedder River with

a photo of Tanya Smith. It was a positive match. The girl in the river was Tanya Smith.

As a sad point of coincidence, Tanya's family lived in the small village of Arnold on the Sumas Prairie, only a few kilometers from the location were her body was found. Terry and Gail Smith had moved their family, Tanya, the oldest, and her younger sister and brother to this quiet village to enjoy the farm life in an area where they could ride their horses.

The difficult duty of notifying Tanya's family fell to Abbotsford Police Sergeant Bill Emery. An experienced officer with twenty years of service and the father of five children, Bill brought both experience and empathy to the sad task at hand.

There is no way to prepare a family for such horrific news. It is tragic when the life of a young person is taken by accident. That same loss becomes incomprehensible when a life is taken through a senseless and vicious criminal act. When the news was told to them, the family was devastated. Little can be done for victim families at these times other than helping bring other family members together for support and keeping them informed of the most recent information and progress. In spite of the fact that Bill Emery was the bearer of such tragic news, this first contact struck a bond of trust that would soon become friendship and help support both the Smith family and the police investigation in the weeks and months that were to follow.

THE JOINT
FORCES TEAM

It did not require a great deal of deliberation to see that the two investigations being pursued by Abbotsford and Chilliwack that morning were connected. The attack on the girls and the subsequent discovery of the body were all part of one extended criminal event, and as such, they needed to be investigated together.

At twelve noon on October 14, 1995, investigators from both the Chilliwack RCMP and the Abbotsford City Police met at the Abbotsford Police office. It was agreed to proceed with a single JFO (joint forces investigation). The joint forces investigation proposal was approved by the management teams of both police agencies, and ten investigators from each agency were immediately dedicated to the JFO team that became known as the Homicide Task Force.

As the teller of these events, my perspective comes from my assignment to lead the investigative team in the role of team commander. As the staff sergeant in charge of the Abbotsford Police Criminal Investigation Branch, I was responsible for the development and conduct of the investigative team. This team was set up under a Major Case Management system. Working closely with the primary investigators and the file coordinators, it was my job to monitor the investigation, prioritizing suspects and investigative strategies to ensure effective deployment of the investigative resources. In this role, I reported to Abbotsford Police and Chilliwack RCMP. These two partner agencies needed to supply the required personnel and equipment to keep the investigation running. The role of team commander provided a unique opportunity to see the investigation unfold from both an operational and an organizational perspective.

Under the Major Case Management protocols, it is recommended that one person should be assigned as the primary investigator and one person should be assigned as the file coordinator. Along with the team commander, the primary investigator and the file coordinator form what is know as a command triangle. This command triangle becomes responsible for the overall management of the investigation and the team. Since two major investigations had been started by the partner agencies, these three main roles had already been assigned by each agency. It was decided that there would be two primary investigators, two file coordinators, and, at least initially, two team commanders.

This kind of role duplication was not the ideal structuring for an investigative team; however, in the politics that existed between police agencies in British Columbia, particularly between city police departments and the Royal Canadian Mounted Police, this kind of organizational compromise happened at the expense of effective operations but for the benefit of political peace.

Political peace was important, and this was a politically sensitive time in the history of the Abbotsford Police Department. It was only ten months earlier, on January 1, 1995, that the Matsqui Police Department had been chosen over the Abbotsford RCMP to continue policing the amalgamated municipalities of Abbotsford and Matsqui. As a stark contrast, in eastern Canada many city and regional police departments were being taken over by the RCMP in similar municipal amalgamations. The expectation that the RCMP, Canada's national police force, would be the force of choice in a contest with a small municipal agency did not turn out to be the forgone conclusion that many expected.

The Abbotsford chief constable for the last six years at the time of amalgamation was Barry Daniel. A retired RCMP inspector, Barry was acutely aware of the RCMP internal politics and their amalgamation-bid strategies. He had recently allied himself with new Deputy Chief Constable Ian Mackenzie. Ian had come up through the ranks of the Vancouver City Police, gaining his law degree and working extensively on projects relating to provincial policing infrastructures. Both Barry and Ian had worked tirelessly to present the Matsqui Police as a first choice for the community in the amalgamation bid. Had it not been for their efforts, the City of Abbotsford may have joined the existing "Big 5" RCMP Municipal detachments in the company of Surrey, Burnaby, Richmond, North Vancouver, and Langley. The choice having gone in favor of our small city police department, it was now time to mend fences broken by amalgamation strategies. At the same time it would be important to maintain a level of equality in the partnership we were now facing.

The investigation in this case would clearly be high profile. It always is when young, innocent victims are attacked. Chief Daniel made it very clear that it would be important for the residents of the new City of Abbotsford to know that their newly chosen Abbotsford Police Department was both capable and competent to solve the crime.

To demonstrate organizational competence, it would be equally important for the public to see that the police agencies involved were working together on the case. Bad politics between police agencies had derailed police investigations in the past. We could not afford to let that happen here.

The report of Justice Archie Campbell into the murders committed by Paul Bernardo in Ontario had only recently been made public. Paul Bernardo was a vicious serial rapist and killer. His reign of terror of attacking, abducting and killing Ontario women, took place over a period of several years and crossed a number of different police jurisdictions. In Ontario, the neighboring police agencies involved in the various Bernardo investigations were criticized broadly for failing to share information and cooperate with each other. According to Justice Campbell's report, their lack of cooperation was instrumental in delaying the capture of Bernardo before he could kill again.

From discussion between the partner agencies, it was decided that, because the attack took place in the City of Abbotsford, with the Chilliwack area being the disposal site for the body, Abbotsford Police Department would take the role as lead agency for the investigation. The task force office would be located in the Abbotsford Police Department conference room. Vehicles, radios, and equipment would be provided by each agency on a per-officer basis. The command triangle would be made up of officers from each partner agency performing parallel roles. Politics aside, we needed to make the Joint Forces arrangement work.

As my counterpart, Staff Sergeant Ralph Miller was named Chilliwack RCMP team commander. At the time, Ralph had nearly thirty years of service in the RCMP and was normally in charge of the Chilliwack RCMP General Investigation Section (GIS). With a strong background in data systems, it was agreed that Ralph would undertake the implementation of the Records Management System required to manage the major file. I would oversee the management of daily operational and investigative matters.

Sergeant Bill Emery of the Abbotsford Police was named as one primary investigator, and Corporal Kevin Macleod of the Chilliwack RCMP was identified as the other. Both Bill and Kevin were in charge of investigative sections as part of their regular duties, and both had worked extensively in previous homicide investigations. As a fortunate coincidence, Bill, Kevin, and I had all known each other for many years and had worked together on previous cases. In their roles as primary investigators, Bill and Kevin would be responsible for the complete review of all investigative materials. They would assign tips to various investigators and would receive the completed investigations back. They would oversee evidence collection from both crime scene exhibits and from identified witnesses. Many other investigators would be assigned to the team; however, any and all information on suspects and investigative process needed to clear through the primary investigators.

The file coordinators identified were Constable Jamie Bawtinheimer for the Abbotsford Police and Constable Dave Vince for the Chilliwack RCMP. Both Dave and Jamie were senior constables and experienced criminal investigators. In the critical position of file coordinators, they would be responsible for the documentation and prioritization of incoming tips. They would act as quality assurance for the completed documentation of investigative files as the case progressed. Ultimately, the integrity of the police investigative file can be lost if it cannot be demonstrated that an impeccable system of file management and information maintenance was utilized.

As these Joint Forces Operations (JFO) agreements were being made, and as the team was being set up to conduct the investigation, none of us had any idea just how quickly and how dramatically the dynamics of the investigation would change. We would all soon be driven to an ever-growing level of urgency to capture the killer.

THE FIRST SEVENTY-TWO HOURS

The first seventy-two hours of any homicide investigation are considered critical. These are the hours when crime scenes are examined, autopsies are conducted, and witnesses are located and interviewed. In the first seventy-two hours, vast amounts of information are incoming to the police, and the best opportunity still exists to locate and retrieve evidence, to revive the memories of witnesses involved, and to build the most accurate account of the events.

By four p.m. on the afternoon of October 14, 1995, the investigative team was meeting in the task force conference room. We were sketching out the priorities for the investigative plan that would continue strongly for the next sixty hours. The list of priorities was established:

1.   Misty had been moved from the MSA Hospital to the head trauma unit of the Royal Columbian Hospital in New Westminster. It had been determined that her skull was frac-

tured and her brain was swelling. She was in critical condition and would require immediate surgery to save her life.

Recognizing that she was the only living eyewitness to
the events, we knew she would be perceived by the killer
as a threat to his identity and freedom. As such, she would
require a constant police guard at the hospital. A shift rota-
tion of officers was assigned to twenty-four-hour guard
duty. As part of the guarding, duty officers were given a
tape recorder and directed to tape anything that Misty
might have to say about what had happened.

2. Canvassing of fishermen at the Vedder River established
   that clothing had been found in the bushes. This showed us
   where the body had been dragged down a path and dumped
   into the river in a treed area.
   - Tanya's shoes (Dockers brand) were still not
     located and needed to be searched for further.
   - A white van had been seen in the area near the
     dumpsite earlier that morning with two men
     coming and going.
   - A media release looking for information on the
     missing shoes and the white van was drafted,
     approved, and released.

3. Officers were assigned to continue an ongoing search on
   Bevan Avenue and attempt to establish the exact location
   of the attack on the girls.

4. Investigators were assigned to interview the new friends
   that Misty and Tanya had been out with that evening. What
   was their time line? Whom had they been with? Could the
   killer have been among the group of new friends?

5. Canvassing for witnesses along the route that Tanya and Misty were believed to have walked was assigned to a team of officers.

6. Victim profiles of both Tanya and Misty were assigned, with a priority to look for anyone connected to them that may have been capable of this crime.

7. The ongoing seizure and examination of exhibits would be a job for both the Abbotsford Police and Chilliwack RCMP, Forensic Identification Sections (FIS). Misty's clothing, Tanya's clothing, footprints, and tire marks at the river needed to be meticulously gathered and preserved for future examination.

8. Immediate records searches of parolees and day-release offenders from the local Federal Jail, Matsqui Institution, and the local federal day-parole facility, Sumas Center, were assigned. It had happened all too frequently in the past that this kind of crime was the work of someone recently released or on parole for similar offences. Who was in the area that might fit the profile?

9. Investigators were assigned to attend the autopsy of Tanya Smith, scheduled for October 17, 1995.

10. The database for a file-management system needed to be immediately established. The incoming information would amount to volumes. Beyond the simple indexing of names, the system needed to be established that linked names to vehicles, exhibits, events, and other persons. Database file-management systems with these linkage and cross-referencing features had just begun to come into functional use for major case manage-

ment, and this investigation would become one of the first to utilize a full-scale version of such a system.

ii. A media strategy was developed to ask for public assistance. The facts were released that two young girls had been attacked by a man with a baseball bat somewhere near the schools on Bevan Avenue. The body of Tanya Smith was eventually found at the Vedder Canal, and although badly injured, Misty Cockerill had found her way to the emergency ward. Police had not yet established the exact site of the attack on the girls. We advised the public that the unknown attacker was still at large and warned everyone to be cautious. We asked the media to request public assistance for:

- Information regarding anyone who saw Tanya and Misty on the evening of October 13, 1995, particularly in the area of the attack
- Anyone with any knowledge of how Misty got to the hospital
- Anyone finding Tanya's missing shoes at the Vedder River

The media knew that a homicide like this, with innocent victims and an unknown suspect, would demand ongoing attention. There were so many angles for the media to pursue that the story would gain a life of its own. *Who were the victims, and how are their families being impacted? How is the community reacting in fear of a killer? The killer is still at large. Do the police have any leads? Are the police applying enough resources to work on this crime? When will more information become available?*

As more information became known to the media and the

public, the inflow of tips grew rapidly. Along with regular complaint takers receiving calls, special tips lines were set up in the task force office, and frequently tips and overflow calls were forwarded directly into the tips line. These lines were often so busy that all members on duty were taking calls, including primary investigators and myself as the team commander.

By the morning of October 17, 1995, as the investigation moved into its fourth day, beyond the seventy-two-hour mark, things were starting to find their own rhythm. Most of our twenty-person team had been working sixteen- to twenty-hour days. The need to slow the pace of the investigation was evident. Not that anyone was complaining about the hours; they all knew and accepted that long hours went with the turf. The fact is, in the police culture, being assigned to work on a serious homicide is both the ultimate challenge and the gravest of responsibilities.

Chief Barry Daniel said it in part when he commented, "The outcome of this case could be either our finest hour or our worst nightmare." I know for my team members that it went beyond any feeling of responsibility to make our police departments look good. Most of us were members of the community. Our own families were facing this threat too. We shared a common cause, and that cause was to protect our community from a predator. It would soon become apparent just how profound this common cause was in creating the most dedicated and tireless investigators. So far, here at the seventy-two-hour mark, dedication and stamina had only been tested in the first investigative sprint. They would eventually be proven equally true in the marathon that was to come.

The major pieces of evidence and initial witness location were all in place. The investigative plan was being established to meet the flow of incoming tips. As we looked toward day five and the task priorities, I met with the Primary Investigators Bill Emery and Kevin Macleod to discuss the steps for the day to come.

October 17 started with good news. Misty was regaining full consciousness and becoming more coherent in her account of the events leading up to the attack. With the description provided, we were able to narrow the area down to a couple of blocks on Bevan Avenue across from the school grounds. After operations to pin broken bones in her hands and arm and drilling holes in her skull to relieve the pressure of swelling, doctors were more optimistic that she would recover.

It was clear from the level of interest paid to the daily reports on Misty's progress that she had become more than a normal crime victim to our team of investigators. Everyone was anxious for the well-being of the brave young girl. Her courage and resolve had been demonstrated. She had chosen to stand and fight back to save her friend instead of running away. Beaten almost to death, she had struggled with an incredible will to survive to find the hospital where she fought to remain conscious and report her friend, who was still in trouble. Expressions of relief and satisfaction were evident on the faces of team members to know that she would recover.

Knowing that Misty represented an ongoing threat to the perpetrator as an eyewitness, we remained committed to the twenty-four-hour armed guard at her hospital room. When she was discharged, we would make other arrangements to protect her.

Unknown to Misty, as she was recovering in the head-

trauma unit of the Royal Columbian Hospital, the body of
her good friend Tanya was in the same hospital, undergoing
autopsy downstairs in the pathology department.

UNIQUE HOLDBACK EVIDENCE

Doctors conducting the autopsy discovered that Tanya's wounds were very similar to Misty's. There was evidence of several strikes to the head and defensive wounds to the arms. Although these wounds were as life threatening, Tanya may have survived if she had received medical attention. The cause of death was determined to be drowning. In other words, she was alive but likely not conscious when she arrived at the river, and the act of placing her facedown in the water actually caused her death.

A full forensic autopsy on a homicide victim in a modern hospital such as Royal Columbian Hospital in New Westminster is done by specially trained doctors. In this case it was Dr. Sheila Carlisle, whose goal was to uncover any and all possible evidence of the crime and crime-related acts.

The cause of death, drowning, was determined by water in the victim's lungs.

Abrasions on the victim's back parallel to her spine indicated that her body had been dragged over a rough surface.

Swabbing of the vulva revealed semen that was collected for DNA examination.

In examining the breasts, Dr. Carlisle saw a muted bruising and abrasion believed to be a bite-mark on the right nipple. With this discovery, Dr. David Sweet, a well-known forensic odontologist, was called in to consult. Dr. Sweet attended and confirmed that this was in fact a bite-mark. The mark showed enough unique accidental characteristics to make it identifiable to a specific set of teeth. Dr. Sweet took the necessary steps to preserve a record of the bite characteristics for future comparison. He then performed a special procedure to swab the bite-mark for suspect DNA.

Using a newly developed double-swab technique, Dr. Sweet was able to obtain a saliva sample from the bite-mark that would eventually produce a searchable DNA profile. Considering that Tanya's body had been found floating facedown in the water, it was remarkable that the collection of a saliva sample was even possible.

On the afternoon of October 17, 1995, I met with Bill Emery and Kevin MacLeod. We talked about getting our team back into a shift pattern. We needed to start making provision for regular time off. Just as we finished our planning, a call came in from Constable Kevin Hackett, one of the team members assigned to attend the autopsy. As Constable Hackett recounted the findings of the autopsy, it was clear that this evidence would be significant.

In the world of criminal investigation, real physical evidence, such as fingerprints, DNA, or physical-characteristic matches, are always good news for investigators. They all help to establish points of fact that can be depended upon as certainties in the investigation. When it comes time for court, the judge will generally place a high level of credibility on physical evidence in contrast to the evidence of eyewitnesses, which can be flawed by memory or influenced by things heard from others.

The fact that Tanya died of drowning at the river led to many questions and speculation surrounding why the attacker would take the body of one girl and not the other. Perhaps Misty had gotten up and left the attack site before the attacker could return to remove their bodies. Viciously beating the girls in the initial attack might allow for a defence that there was no premeditation to kill; however, placing the body of an unconscious girl facedown in the water carries a much stronger tone of premeditation. Premeditation being one of the components distinguishing between first- and second-degree murder is extremely important in any homicide case.

The DNA in the form of semen would serve both to corroborate that the attacker had finished the sexual assault on Tanya that Misty had witnessed the start of. DNA, like fingerprints, would also serve as a strong point of positive identification of a suspect if we could find one. Causing a person's death while committing a sexual assault also elevates a homicide to first-degree rather than second-degree murder.

DNA from the semen would be excellent evidence. Unfortunately, comparisons would not be quick. At this time in 1995, forensic DNA collection and comparison had only recently been accepted by the courts. In their efforts to ensure that DNA comparison for forensic purposes was developed in a scientific environment that could withstand challenges in court, the Crime Detection laboratories were extremely meticulous in their development of procedures for comparison. As a result, the typical turnaround for a DNA-sample comparison was four to six months. All DNA work would prove to be a slow process.

The fractures to the skull and arms showed that once he finished his attack on Misty, he continued in a similar fashion on Tanya. The abrasions on the back were indicators that the body had been dragged across a hard surface somewhere. Finally, the bite-mark on the right nipple was a unique and unusual addition to a homicide. As a bonus, the bite-mark and the DNA from saliva collected could provide additional points for positive identification once a suspect was located.

As Kevin Hackett recounted the evidence located that afternoon, it was clear that the bite-mark would serve as an excellent piece of holdback information. In a police investigation, holdback information is a fact about the crime that could be known only to the perpetrator and the police investigators. Protecting holdback evidence as secret and eventually obtaining a confession or reference to knowledge of the holdback from a suspect is generally considered incriminating. At the very least, it is intimate knowledge of the crime that an accused would need to explain.

At 4:30 p.m. on the afternoon of October 17, 1995, the investigative team gathered for the regular afternoon briefing. All of the physical evidence was an excellent advance in the investigation at this early point in time. Only four days into the investigation, we already had semen for DNA comparison and a bite-mark. Either of these could positively identify the suspect. All we had to do was find the right suspect to compare the DNA and dental impression against.

As we briefed the team that day, it was emphasized that the bite-mark information needed to be closely guarded and shared only on a need-to-know basis. Anyone identified as a strong suspect could be offered the opportunity to be positively cleared through DNA comparison or through dental impression.

Being able to positively clear suspects in any criminal investigation is a huge bonus for investigators. Without objective physical evidence to clear suspects, elimination is an ambiguous process demanding background investigations to verify alibis. In some investigations without physical evidence, suspects cannot be conclusively cleared.

Even though we were past seventy-two hours and some excellent evidence was in hand, we had still not located the exact site of the attack on Tanya and Misty. Searching for this site would continue to be a priority.

The drop site where the body had been placed in the river was made extremely clear in contrast to the attack site. A muddy path through the trees that led up to gently sloping beach was clearly the approach taken. It was defined by a clear set of drag marks and boot prints through the mud in the middle of the trail. Items of Tanya's clothing were randomly tossed and hanging on the bushes on either side of the trail. It was clear that the attacker was not trying to hide anything; although, as shared with the media, we were still looking for Tanya's shoes, a secondary search of the body dumpsite that included cutting back blackberry bushes had located a set of sandals. We later learned that these were the shoes Misty had loaned Tanya prior to leaving the house. Tanya's Dockers-brand shoes would be found in Misty's bedroom.

FIRST GLIMPSE OF THE SHADOW

On October 18, 1995, as the investigation moved into its fifth day, the flow of tips from the public was increasing. Misty was fully conscious and feeling stronger, and Misty's mother had to tell her that Tanya had not survived the attack. Up to this point, Misty had been sending many of the flowers she received to Tanya's room. Investigators on guard at the hospital that day once again saw the strength of the young lady who had the courage to fight back against her attacker. As she tearfully accepted the loss of her friend, she went on that same day to provide more details of the attack site. Misty told investigators that she had struggled from the attack site, along a chain-link fence, and eventually lying down to rest in a garden. Getting up later, she found the emergency ward entrance to the hospital and walked in under her own steam.

At 11:09 a.m., October 18, 1995, Kevin Macleod and I were in the task force office reviewing files when Kevin picked up an incoming call on the tips line. Kevin embarked on a four-minute conversation in which he was trying to talk a subject into coming to the police office. When the call suddenly terminated, Kevin explained that the male caller claimed that he was the one who had helped Misty get to the hospital, and he just wanted us to know. In spite of Kevin's attempts to persuade him to come in, the caller stated that he did not trust cops and would not come to the office. He terminated the call.

Similar to all police departments, the incoming telephone lines to the Abbotsford Police were tape-recorded and traced to show the location where calls originated. A search to obtain a copy of this call revealed that the recording system had not been connected to the task force tip lines. Fortunately, the external-location trace was working. The call was determined to have originated from a pay telephone outside of the "Circle K" Shell Gas station in Abbotsford.

Investigators were immediately dispatched to the "Circle K" station. No witnesses could be found at the scene. The pay phone used by the caller was on the exterior wall of the station, outside the view of the security surveillance camera.

We could not afford to have tape recording fail on these kinds of calls. Temporary tape recorders were patched onto the tip lines in the task force office to cover future calls until the main system could be extended to cover the phones. As this was being done, Kevin related his impression of the caller. He sounded like the typical redneck with a criminal past and a chip on his shoulder. Was he telling the truth? Did he really take Misty to the hospital? Kevin wasn't sure. The tip was written up and filed.

As the morning progressed, team members working with new additional information from Misty were searching the area behind the MSA Hospital. Just after noon, one of the Abbotsford Police dog handlers, Constable Linda McLennan, located a grassy area on the corner of the parking lot. She tied up her dog and crawled through the grass on her hands and knees, carefully parting the grass. As a payoff for this extra effort, Linda located a broken hoop earring that had been knocked from Misty's head during the attack. The grassy area proved to be the exact location of the attack. Unfortunately, following two days of heavy rain, the earring would be the only evidence still present. Everything else had been washed away or otherwise removed.

The day progressed with additional developments. A farmer on the Sumas Prairie had located an aluminum baseball bat in one of the ditches next to the roads that led to the Vedder Canal dyke. The bat found on the surface of grass in the ditch had obviously been thrown there recently. The bat was seized and retained as an exhibit. It was examined for blood and tissue with negative results. The roadway beside the ditch was one of the main routes the perpetrator could have taken to get to or leave the dyke.

Many unanswered questions surrounded the exhibit. Was this the attack weapon? If so, why wasn't it discarded with the clothing at the dumpsite? If it was taken from the attack site and not thrown away at the dumpsite, why throw it away at all? These were all good questions to contemplate, but we wouldn't have more time to think about it today.

As 4:30 p.m. briefing approached on October 18, 1995, the task force office was humming with activity. The task force office was twenty-feet wide and forty-feet long with table workstations down the center and along both walls. Case-management computers populated the far end of the room, and report-writing stations lined the walls. Investigators returning for the afternoon briefing visited and exchanged information of the day's events. Today, as a result of Constable McLennan's diligence, we had confirmed the attack site, and thanks to our farmer friend, we had a possible attack weapon. All of this added to the list of what we knew about the crime, and it all helped to shape the foundation of our case.

In the flurry of late-afternoon activities, one of the tip lines was ringing and I picked it up. Barely able to hear the male caller on the line, I waved my hand in the air, gesturing for quiet. Before I could switch the tape recorder on, I heard the male say, "I know where the murder happened." I hit the record switch and was about to respond with a question when the male caller continued. I silenced my response in deference to the caller's obvious desire to speak.

He continued. "Beside a walkway that runs north and south on a grassy knoll behind trees."

I was able to interject and ask, "Okay, sir. Where are you getting this from?"

He responded, "I'm the killer. Her right nipple tasted pretty good." The caller hung up, leaving me alone on the open line with my mind racing, mildly shocked, and attempting to fully absorb the scope and implications of what had just been said. This had to be our bad guy. Who else would know about the bite on her right nipple? Only hours earlier had we established that the attack site was as he had described: next to a north-south sidewalk behind trees. With the tape recorder still running, almost in disbelief, I uttered the words, "Wow, s***. Let's get a trace on this."

As I shut off the recorder, the entire room went silent,

and eyes were focused on me. The police members who had worked with me often joked that they could read my expressions like a book. I don't know what expression showed on my face at that moment, but whatever it was, my colleagues knew that what I had just heard must be serious.

I rewound the tape and played the team what I had heard. Expressions of disbelief and concern prevailed in the room. The communications sergeant returned and announced that the call had originated from the pay phone across from the MSA hockey arena. We immediately scrambled eight unmarked cars into the area. The instructions to officers attending were clear: check everything that moves in the area of the phone booth. I immediately made a working copy of the tape and held the original for exhibits.

When I attended to the area of the MSA arena, I could see our teams at work, talking to people in the parking lots and on the sidewalk. The problem was that the phone booth in question was on the edge of Centennial Park across the street from the MSA arena. It was a beautiful afternoon, and both the park and the arena were full of activity. We couldn't possibly check everyone, but there had to be a witness somewhere.

Our forensic identification members attended and dusted the telephone for fingerprints. After an hour of street checks and interviews of people in the area, we walked away without a witness. No one we spoke to had seen anyone at that phone booth.

At briefing that afternoon, we played back the tape several times. Who were we dealing with here? It had been twenty-four hours since we'd learned about the bite-mark and deemed it to be holdback. Now, we had a caller telling us that he knew were the murder happened, he described the attack site, and he demonstrated knowledge of the holdback with "her right nipple tasted pretty good."

The caller had to be the killer himself or someone to whom the killer had confided. Why would the killer himself want to phone the police? Whatever his reason, he sounded like he was enjoying himself. When he made his final comment, "Her right nipple tasted pretty good," there was a distinctive lilt in his voice that made it sound as if he were about to laugh.

Was this the same guy Kevin MacLeod had spoken to earlier, claiming that he had taken Misty to the hospital? Kevin didn't think the voice sounded the same, but he wasn't sure.

At briefing that same afternoon, investigators shared details of subjects interviewed in the door-to-door canvassing in the area of the attack site. More information was emerging. Shortly after midnight on October thirteenth, an elderly lady living in an apartment building that bordered Bevan Avenue and overlooked the attack site stepped out onto her sundeck. She did so after hearing what sounded like two girls screaming. When she looked out, she saw a full-sized sedan proceeding west on Bevan Avenue and then making a U-turn, stopping in the sidewalk area behind the Extended Care Unit. The car only stopped briefly and then departed the area. She had dismissed the screaming as kids fooling around and did not call police.

Another team interviewed a security guard working just after midnight on October 13. He was on mobile patrol in a shopping center to the east of the Extended Care Unit on Bevan three blocks from the attack site. He recalled hearing screams as well. He drove his vehicle west on Bevan to the area where the screams were heard and made a U-turn. He could see a male walking east on the opposite side of the cedar hedge as he proceeded to drive east along Bevan and back to his shopping mall duties. He also dismissed the screams as kids fooling around.

Owing to our prolonged activities at the phone booth at MSA Arena, briefing went on late that afternoon. Shortly after six p.m., the duty sergeant entered the task force office and advised that the Abbotsford Police 911 dispatcher had just received a very disturbing call.

A recording of this 911 call was obtained and played:

Call 6:08 p.m. October 18, 1995, to Abbotsford Police 911 Operator

Operator: "911 emergency. Do you need police, fire, or ambulance?"

Caller: "Police."

Operator: "Pardon me?"

Caller: "Police."

Operator: "You've got the police."

Caller: "Your guys do a real thorough job, but do you think I would be stupid enough to leave fingerprints behind when I make a phone call?"

Operator: "I can hardly hear you."

Caller: "Do you think I would be stupid enough to leave fingerprints behind when I make a phone call?"

Operator: "Hello … Hello …"

Hearing the caller's voice, it was clearly the same person as the previous recording. His remark was obviously a reference to dusting the MSA arena phone for prints. Apparently, the killer had been there, watching from a location close enough to know that we had dusted the telephone booth for prints.

When we asked for the address where the call had originated, we learned once again that the technology of our tracing and recording systems was not foolproof. Typically, an incoming 911 call from anywhere within the police jurisdiction will display on the dispatch screen showing the address where the call originates. In this case, there was no such call display and, at least for the moment, no explanation for the system's failure. Other incoming 911 calls were all displaying properly. Did this person have a way of bypassing our 911-location system, or was this just a technical glitch?

As the team discussed the details and meaning of the most recent call, the duty Sergeant once again advised us that the 911 operator had just received another call. This one was even more disturbing.

The call was copied and reviewed:

Call 6:29 p.m. October 18, 1995, to Abbotsford Police 911 Operator

Operator: "911 emergency. Do you need police, fire, or ambulance?"
Caller: "Police"
Operator: "Go ahead."
Caller: "Are you having trouble finding the killer?"

Operator:	"Ah…I'm not sure. Do you want to provide information through to our members?"
Caller:	"No. I'm the one."
Operator:	"You're the."
Caller:	"I'm giving you the chance to try and find me. I'll be driving around looking for someone else."
Operator:	"And what is your name?"
Caller:	"Just to let you know who I am, Tanya's right nipple tasted really good."
Operator:	"And what is your name?"

This time the call-location feature of the 911 system did work, and the call was traced to the telephone booth at the Ventura Grocery Store, a convenience store a few blocks from the Abbotsford Police office. Police teams scrambled to attend the area, and in spite of many possible witnesses in the area near the scene of the call, no one saw anyone at the telephone booth.

The circumstances we were facing did not require further clarification. The threat was real, and we needed to respond.

RAISING THE STAKES

In a matter of a few hours, because of three phone calls, our investigation had gone from a standard homicide investigation, where the risk of repeat attack lurks in the back of everyone's mind, to a full-blown overt threat to kill again. Worse yet, the threat was coming from an individual so bold that he was inventing his own game with the police.

As I briefed Chief Daniel and Inspector Skrine of the Chilliwack RCMP on the developments, there was grave concern that things were going to get out of hand. Would we soon have another body to deal with? The threat was too real to be taken lightly. Moreover, the fact that our perpetrator obviously had a vehicle expanded the range of the threat. With a vehicle and the ability to travel, he did not have to restrict his activities to Abbotsford or Chilliwack. He was a threat to the entire Fraser Valley of British Columbia and farther.

In modern police investigations, when faced with this kind of unusual or bizarre behavior, the police are ill advised to rely solely on their own experiences to inform their decision-making. Consulting with external sources provides the opportunity for expert opinion, new ideas, and alternate perspectives. In this case, we turned to Dr. Mike Webster.

Dr. Webster, a well-known psychologist with a specialty in conflict management, had frequently been used by police in Canada and the United States. He often provided advice on suspect behavior during active investigations. What was the suspect doing now? What might he be expected to do next? What should or shouldn't the police do?

As a resident of Abbotsford, Mike was well known to our police department as both a friend and a consultant. As a former professional wrestler and B.C. Lions football player, Mike's post-sports career had taken him into the field of psychology, in which he earned his Ed.D. With a doctorate and a keen interest in policing, he had joined the Royal Canadian Mounted Police for a brief time prior to becoming a full-time psychologist and consultant. Phone calls to Dr. Webster confirmed our fears: Overt interaction, such as these phone calls, by a suspect are unusual and unpredictable. On the positive side, the fact that he seemed to be getting some level of satisfaction out of his bizarre phone interaction indicated that he might be satisfied, at least in the short-term, to get his thrills through threatening and taunting the police.

We reviewed tapes of the three phone calls further, and it was clear from the tone and inflection that our suspect was excited. There was almost a singsong quality to the messages, with raised pitch as the phrases ended. Was he using a disguised voice? It was time for another expert opinion. The tapes would be taken to the linguistics department at the University of British Columbia to determine if language and voice experts could provide additional clues.

As an investigative team, we discussed the implications of the new turn of events. What did the telephone contacts mean to the investigation? The killer had clearly upped the stakes; the threat was real.

Everyone agreed that, on the positive side, every time the attacker made contact, he exposed himself to the risk of being caught, and that was a good thing. Not only did these exposures pose opportunities to catch him; they provided points of reference for the elimination of other persons whom we needed to clear as suspects. In other words, if a suspect could supply an alibi for where he or she was at the time of the attack, or at the times of any of the three phone calls, we could use those times as points of elimination. What about the voice? If it wasn't disguised, if he was using his real voice, someone could recognize it.

RAISING THE ALARM

On the negative side of the equation, the very real threat had to be shared with the public. From a policing perspective, an officer never wants to see his community living in fear. Understandably, the level of public anxiety as a result of the attack on the two girls was high. One young girl had been murdered, and now we were going to add to that by sharing the threatening calls. The public had a right to know, and the police had an obligation to raise the alarm and give warning.

The media on the case were already in high gear. Sharing information about threatening phone calls from the attacker would only escalate things further. In a carefully worded release to the media, the public were advised and alerted.

Police investigating the murder of Tanya Smith and attempted murder of Misty Cockerill had received phone calls from a male claiming to be the killer. From the content of the calls, police believe that the caller is the person responsible for the murder. The calls are of a threatening nature, and police are cautioning the public to take extra precautions to protect their safety.

THE COMMUNITY MOURNS A CHILD

On October 19, 1995, as the media were being advised of the escalated threat, Misty, although still in the hospital, had improved enough to work with an RCMP forensic artist Corporal Cameron Pye. Misty completed a composite that we would later release to the media.

First composite drawing of the suspect

The news media release played frequently and drew national media attention. Tanya's family and members of the community participated in candlelight vigils and marches.

As Tanya's funeral approached, the tragedy and the threat remained ever present.

On October 21, 1995, to assist in the surveillance and covert filming of Tanya Smith's funeral, the RCMP Surveillance team, "Special O," was called upon. They would videotape the coming and going of both cars and people at the funeral.

It was a rainy, cold day typical of the fall season. A huge crowd of family, friends, and supportive community members gathered for the funeral service. While the service proceeded inside, surveillance team members outside combed the parking areas, taking down license numbers of vehicles. As the crowd left the church, everyone was recorded on video.

Recording of funeral services is a common practice in homicide cases. This is done because it is not unheard of for a suspect or someone identified as suspicious to attend a victim's funeral. The surveillance and filming went by without any suspicious or unusual activity noted. It was simply a family and a community grieving together for a lost child.

The funeral procession left the church and proceeded to the small Mennonite cemetery a few miles away. Tanya's grave would eventually be marked with a granite headstone embossed with a photo of Tanya and an engraving of sunflowers. A short inscription and the words "Our Sunflower, Forever in our Hearts" would frame the stone.

HE LIKES WHAT HE IS DOING

After Tanya's funeral, the routines of the Homicide Task Force returned to a day-to-day rhythm. With an organized system of recording incoming tips from the public and assigning tips to investigative teams, shifts were established, and daily briefings became part of that routine. There were two full-time tip takers feeding incoming tips to file coordinators. The incoming volume was daunting but under control.

Investigators on the team were finally getting occasional days off on weekends, and on Halloween night, October 31, 1995, many of the team were home with their young families for a much-deserved night off. Halloween in Abbotsford was going to be pretty quiet. With the threat of a killer on the loose, there was not a lot of visible trick-or-treating going on. As with most nights as of late, after dark the streets were noticeably empty of pedestrian traffic.

The call came in at 9:10 p.m., again to the Abbotsford Police 911 Operator:

Operator:	911 Emergency, do you need police, fire, or ambulance?
Caller:	Police.
Operator:	What is your emergency?
Caller:	Tonight I'm not going to bite her right nipple. I'm going to eat her f****** c***.

The call was traced to a telephone booth outside of Gigi's Sports Bar, a local pub close to the freeway entrance. Patrol officers arriving at the scene found the phone booth vacant; however, a witness nearby was able to provide description of a beige Granada that had been parked in front of the booth moments before the police arrived.

A team of detectives was called out to listen to the latest—call number four. It was clearly the same voice, and the caller referenced the bite-mark once again, confirming his credibility. But this time, as he spoke his single-sentence message, he clearly became more excited, more intense, and his voice rose to a squeaky crescendo. We speculated that he might have been masturbating as he made the call. At the very least, it was evident that he got some kind of perverse pleasure as he spoke to the operator. Dr. Webster's comments about the suspect enjoying his post-crime activity continued to ring true. As investigators, our speculation that he would continue to use the bite-mark to verify his own identity was also proving true. This would be another call and location for the experts to examine.

As it turned out, Dr. Mike Webster was not the only help we would have in psychological profiling. As an addition to our investigative team, the RCMP Behavioral Science

Unit from Ottawa came to Abbotsford. They would assist by developing a psychological profile of the attacker. The profiling team of Inspector Ron McKay, Inspector Glen Woods, Sergeant Keith Davidson, and Dr. Peter Collins were intensely interested in determining the profile of a suspect such as ours. Admittedly, few criminals play the game of calling to taunt the police.

The science of criminal profiling evolves from basic assumptions regarding human behavior.

- First, a person's behavior is a direct reflection of needs they are trying to satisfy.
- Second, past behavior of an individual is the best predictor of that person's future behavior.
- Third, the examination of past behaviors of criminals committing a certain crime-types, along with the examination of their common traits, can provide a model for criminal profiling and predicting.

A psychological profile can indicate personal descriptors with respect to gender, age, race, education, intelligence, social status, employment, marital status, and criminal history profiled against various types of criminal acts.

A great deal of social and psychological research has gone into criminal profiling, and this research provides the basis upon which profiling assessments are made. Much of the research comes from after-the-fact debriefings of real criminals and reviews of the crimes they have committed. With data from thousands of crimes in hand, trends and commonalities become apparent. To illustrate the point, let's say that out of ten thousand armed robberies, it has been established that 80 percent were committed by white males between the ages of eighteen and twenty-seven; it would be reasonable to predict that out of any given armed robbery, there is a high likelihood that the suspect will be a white male between eighteen and twenty-seven years of age.

Some of the most interesting profiling information comes from post-crime interviews with persons diagnosed as psychopaths or sociopaths. These interviews and case studies yielded characteristics to help profilers determine if the perpetrator is among the percentage of criminals who live their lives without the restrictions of conscience or guilt to subdue their violent behaviors. These psychopaths and sociopaths are often the persons responsible for the most horrific of crimes.

Within the science of criminal profiling, there is a reliable level of predictability, but not always, and the science certainly encounters more difficulty when the behavior being observed is radically uncommon to what one might consider "normal" criminal behavior. As the investigation progressed, psychological profiling would play an important role, but it would not all be in the traditional practice of profiling.

At the same time, as the psychological profiling was initiated, we started discussions with Inspector Kim Rosomo of the Vancouver City Police. Kim had recently earned his PhD at Simon Fraser University, and in his thesis he had created a system for the geographic profiling of criminals. Based upon principles similar to psychological profiling, geographic profiling looks for the predictability of where criminals will commit their offences in relation to where they work and live.

Similar to the hunting patterns of predatory animals, Dr.

Rosomo had proven through the study of historical data on criminals and their offence locations that a correlation existed between the location of a crime and where the suspect lived or worked. The reliability of a geographic-profile model increases with the number of confirmed suspect offences or contact locations available. We had the crime scene, the body dumpsite, and the location of three phone booths to work with, and that would be enough for a start.

WORKING WITH THE MEDIA

Having a completed composite sketch, it was decided that along with the information regarding the telephone calls, the composite would be released to the public.

The linguistics department at the University of British Columbia provided their opinion on the voice tapes, confirming that the voice was consistent from one call to the next. They did not believe that the voice was being disguised, and, confirming another suspicion, there were no characteristics indicating an accent or ethnic origin.

With this information in hand, it was decided that we would release an edited copy of the voice tapes to the media. The release was made in hopes that someone would recognize the voice and call in to identify the killer.

The news releases would be the assignment of our appointed media liaison person, Constable Elly Sawchuk. A member of the Abbotsford Police Department, Elly had a straightforward and tough-minded approach balanced effectively by attractive features and a ready smile. She would need all this and more as she built her media contacts and credibility in the midst of the frenzy.

On November 6, 1995, at a packed press conference, a composite drawing of the suspect was displayed in the background while Elly played an edited version of the suspect phone calls for the media. The request for public assistance was made: *This is what the suspect may look like. This is the voice of the suspect. If you recognize either or both, please call the police tip line. Or if you want to hear the voice again, call the special 800 number.*

The special 800 number allowed callers to listen to the edited voice tapes played over and over again. Unknown to callers, it was set up to identify the telephone numbers of those calling to listen. Anyone who called to listen more than three times was considered a person of interest and was flagged for interview by investigators.

Was it possible that our bad guy was so worked up that he would call to listen to himself over and over again, reliving his glory with each phone call? We could only hope. In many ways, an investigation of this nature is similar to fishing; all you can do is strategically bait your hook with your best guess as to what the predator will be attracted to, then optimistically wait for the tug of success. Will that tug come as a tip from someone with new critical information, or will it be an outright strike of the predator himself, surfacing to be seen with an opportunity for capture? This is where the whole police team needs to be alert to the possibilities. The more lines you have in the water, the better your chances.

The only thing not included in the edited tapes was the reference to the bite-mark. As much as was possible, we needed to protect this piece of knowledge. The bite to the nipple was the secret known only to the suspect and us. As the investigation progressed, it would continue to be the validation and his signature for communication.

As an investigative team, we had given serious consideration before releasing the tapes. We could have told the public that we had received the threatening calls, but there was more to be gained by being strategic and selective. It was important to keep the public focused on certain critical details and provide opportunities to make linkages to information they may not be aware they have. These linkages are the culmination of the thinking process that creates witness awareness of knowledge critical to the police investigation. Normally, police do not share specific evidence that will later be produced in court as evidence. The exception here was based on the notion that sharing the information offered the clear opportunity to identify the suspect.

Our strategy for the release of the tapes was founded on the simple principle of voice recognition. We all know the voices of those close *to* us. These voices are ingrained in our memories, so much so that when a close friend or relative calls, they need not tell us who is calling. After very few words, we recognize the voice; our ears are attuned to the tone, pitch, inflection, and cadence of their voices.

Knowing that this was our suspect's voice, these tapes were our best hope for identification. Some friend, acquaintance, or relative would hear the recordings on the news and call in to identify our killer.

As the news of the threatening phone calls and the composite drawing hit the media, news interest went from intense to relentless, evolving into a news story that was gaining interest at national and international levels.

As news reporters canvassed citizens in the community to gain perspective, it was clear from their responses that people were afraid to go out alone at night. Families were afraid for the safety of their children. Uniformed police officers patrolling Abbotsford noticed it too, with a reduction in pedestrian traffic to near zero after dark and more frequent calls to attend to suspicious circumstances. The community was going to live under the shadow of threat for many months to come. In retrospect, this was a good thing inasmuch as it reduced the number of available targets for the attacker if he was out looking again.

BUILDING THE BIG TEAM

With the additional media attention, our Homicide Task Force office was flooded with calls. Huge volumes of tips were coming in from a public anxious to see the threat dealt with. With an escalated level of threat and the associated increase in tips, the response of the investigation needed to be raised. With only twenty investigators working, we were not going to be able to keep up.

Chief Constable Daniel attended the meeting of all British Columbia police chiefs. These monthly meetings consisted of all municipal police, including the officers in charge of the large RCMP detachments and chief constables of all city police departments. Chief Daniel briefed the police leaders, outlined the escalated threat, and the common threat that was posed by the individual at large in our communities. At the end of the meeting, a commitment was made. All of the police agencies present agreed to provide personnel to supplement the investigative team.

In my opinion, this decision and commitment by police

leaders from the RCMP and Municipal Police Forces was one of the proudest and most defining moments for police cooperation in British Columbia. A common threat to our communities was identified and acknowledged. Police leaders throughout the Fraser Valley changed their own organizational priorities to provide the human resources to deal with it. As the pledges for personnel were met, an additional fifty-five investigators joined the Homicide Task Force Team over the next two weeks. The police agencies of:

Richmond RCMP

Surrey RCMP

Burnaby RCMP

Langley RCMP

North Vancouver RCMP

Vancouver City Police

Delta City Police

New Westminster City Police

West Vancouver City Police

The Coordinated Law Enforcement Unit

Corrections Service of Canada

All of these agencies provided much-needed investigators and the physical resources of vehicles and radios for the team. Along with these added team members, we frequently called upon the specialized services of the RCMP Special "O" Surveillance Section and Vancouver Police Strike Force.

The addition of these investigators could not have come at a better time. Things were really starting to perk. New tips on persons of interest were being called in by the hundreds every day: men who looked like the composite drawing or who sounded like the voice on the tape and men with a history for sex assault. We quickly found the need to develop a prioritization system to categorize our tips. We needed to make sure we looked at the best possibilities first.

Tips were given a point designation if they contained certain criteria:

1.   Sounds like the voice on the tape
2.   Looks like the composite drawing
3.   Linked some way to ether Misty or Tanya
4.   Has past record for violence or sexual assault
5.   Linked to the area of the attack site
6.   Linked to the area of the dumpsite

Obviously, the more criteria the suspect fit, the higher the tip score and priority for investigation. Under this tip scoring system, many tips were set aside for later review.

ANOTHER COMPOSITE OF THE KILLER

As the media interest continued, numerous calls came in from well-meaning persons offering their help. Specialty search dogs, private investigators, persons with sophisticated metal-detection equipment, and psychics all called to offer their assistance.

For the most, part these folks were thanked; however, if they could not offer some immediate and direct contribution, they were turned away.

On November 15, as the team commander, I received one such offer of help that initially sparked suspicion. The man on the telephone identified himself as Robert Exter; he claimed that he was the composite artist the FBI had utilized at the beginning of the infamous *Unabomber* case. Now living on Vancouver Island with his family, Exter advised that he had been following our investigation through the media, and he had concerns regarding the composite drawing we had released. Pointing to his experience as both a portrait artist and a forensic artist, he wanted to let us know that the composite we released to the media was, in his expert opinion, anatomically incorrect. Curious as to how he could make such a statement, I asked him to clarify. He expounded, saying that the human face has a relational set of proportions, and these proportions are generally in balance with each other. In the case of our composite, the forehead was too large and the eyes too wide part. Normal people just don't have those proportions in their features.

Exter offered to come to Abbotsford at his own expense and see if he could produce a better or at least more proportional drawing.

After reviewing some faxed copies of his references and checking with contacts at the Sacramento Police Department, I was satisfied that Mr. Exter was authentic.

After considerable discussion with the team, it was decided that we should let him make a second attempt at a composite drawing. Not to take away from the previous expert efforts of Cameron Pye, but Misty was much further along in her recovery now and was far more lucid. We would let Misty decide when she was finished which of the composites best depicted the attacker.

Prior to proceeding, we consulted with Misty's doctors and asked about the reliability of her memory of the attack. The neurologist advised that anything that happened during or after the attack could be in question, but he believed that Misty's pre-attack memory should be accurate. She should be able to describe her attacker.

On November 16, Exter attended at the task force office.

Misty had sufficiently recovered to meet with him. By the end of the day, Misty and Exter had produced a new composite. Misty rated the likeness a nine out of possible ten points, and we were satisfied that it should become a news release to the media.

16 NOV 95   Exter

Second composite drawing of the suspect

The next day, November 17, 1995, as Misty and her family were placed into the witness protection program, the new composite drawing was released to the media.

The media, hungry for any new details or developments, were quick to give our new composite drawing large-scale exposure. With the exposure came another enormous wave of tips from hundreds of people who knew a lookalike. The drawing was going to be another real tip maker, which is not always a good thing.

RED HERRING

For the task force team, our morning and afternoon briefings were our best forum for group communications. We could always tell when something hot hit the tip line. Before it ever made it to the floor of the briefing room, everyone knew that something was up.

On the morning of November 22, 1995, hundreds of new tips came in because of the new composite. The massive influx of tips was not unusual in and of itself; however, there was a particularly interesting individual identified by three different callers.

The man identified, George Evenden, was known to police. We had a mug shot on file, and placing it next to the composite drawing, one would almost think he had posed for the composite artist. Besides being a strong lookalike to the composite, tipsters provided other compelling circumstantial information potentially linking him to the crime-fact pattern.

Prior to George Evenden arising as a suspect, the investigative team had pulled all outstanding sexual assaults that had happened in the past five years in the Abbotsford area. Several interesting cases were discovered. From the victims in those cases, two women picked Evenden out of photo lineups as their attacker. Much to our surprise, Misty did not.

Evenden became the top suspect. Teams of investigators were set up to gather information on his past, and surveillance teams tracked his movement to establish daily activities and associates. As these processes were going on in the field, warrants were prepared at the task force office. We would need a warrant for his DNA, a special purpose warrant for his dental impression, and warrants to search his residence.

On the early morning of December 1, 1995, Evenden was arrested at his residence and held in custody for the sexual assault of one of the women who had identified him out of the photo lineup. Without an identification from Misty, there was not enough evidence to make an arrest or charge for the attacks on Misty and Tanya. Those charges would need to wait until after we had the chance to compare DNA and the bite-mark.

Immediately upon arrest, Evenden fiercely denied involvement in any of the crimes. Much to our surprise, he was completely cooperative in providing blood samples for DNA testing, as well as dental impression for comparison to the bite-mark. His voice certainly did not sound like the phone tapes, and with his cooperative attitude, he reacted as an innocent person would be expected.

We were beginning to believe that we might have the wrong man. Bite-mark impressions and DNA needed to be compared to be certain.

In spite of the fact that we were trying to keep a lid on the suspect, the media discovered that we had a man in custody and were relentless in their pursuit of more information and leads.

In the police community, word was out that we had a hot suspect, and many were already saying that we had our guy.

Unsure as to whether we had our killer, we did not want to offer false hope to the community. We needed to proceed quickly with the DNA and bite-mark tests. Unfortunately, in 1995, DNA tests, even for an emergency turnaround, took three months. The bite-mark comparison results would weigh heavily.

We called upon forensic expert Dr. David Sweet, who attended and obtained the dental impression from Evenden.

As we awaited the result of the dental impressions, I was called to a meeting with the Abbotsford chief and the officer in charge of Chilliwack RCMP. Both agreed that we had the right suspect and suggested that it was time to start sending people back to their agencies. I had not expected this conversation to take place, and, after a great deal of debate, the bosses relented, for the moment at least. We were only one month into the investigation, and both partner agencies had clearly begun to feel the pinch of the huge draw on their personnel. With the number of investigators on one task force, other crimes were going uninvestigated. Both Chilliwack and Abbotsford were operating with short staffs. The priority of the case needed to be restated and understood.

After extensive discussion of the evidence and the suspect, it was decided that we would wait until after the bite-mark results came back before we made any moves to reduce the investigative team. There were plenty of additional persons of interest who needed to be interviewed and eliminated. The investigation would continue on these persons.

It was agreed on the team that we could not slow down just because of a good "possible suspect" in custody.

After four days, on December 5, 1995, Dr. Sweet called us to advise that he had eliminated Evenden as the person responsible for the bite-mark. Since the bite-mark was such a critical piece of the fact pattern in this case, for the investigative team it amounted to an almost certain elimination. The two sets of bootprints at the dumpsite near the drag marks were the only physical evidence that might support an alternate suspect theory. Could there have been two suspects or, possibly after the attack, an accomplice? Misty certainly only saw one suspect. There was only one voice calling, claiming, "I'm the one," and that voice did not sound at all like Evenden.

This kind of conundrum in police investigations is not uncommon. Some evidence points to a person as a suspect, and other evidence clearly points away. Good objectivity in police work is defined by the ability of investigators to keep an open mind to alternate theories and physical evidence that might not be a fit. Trying to make the facts fit the theory or stubbornly insisting that alternate scenarios are impossible can be fatal to the successful conclusion of a case. The courts are very conscious that loss of objectivity happens.

On this topic, Canadian Supreme Court Justice David Watt once commented, "When you play fast and loose with the law and the intent and spirit of what the courts perceive as principled behavior, you stand to lose the case you most want to win because the trial of the accused is merely a side show. The trial of the investigation is the main event."

With the result of the bite-mark elimination in hand, we

were able to convince all the partner agencies that we needed to continue with the investigation.

Unfortunately for Mr. Evenden, the bite-mark elimination did not deal with the fact that two other women had picked him out of the photo lineup. He would need to remain in custody until the DNA made a positive elimination.

As we all waited for DNA results, the investigation continued. With thousands of tips awaiting investigation, the job became unglamorous police work. Nobody but the cops in the trenches really knows about the daily task of eliminating one subject of interest after another. Enormously time-consuming, many question if this apparently non-productive work really needs to be done. Any officer who has been to court on one of these major unknown-suspect homicides will tell you most certainly it does.

Once you do have a subject charged, you need to be able to stand up in court and satisfy the judge that every effort was made to eliminate the possibility of alternate suspects or even additional suspects. In this case we had a minor piece of evidence that could point to two suspects, or perhaps even a second suspect involved after the fact. Diligent elimination of all the possibilities was a must.

On January 26, 1996, the Vancouver Crime Detection Laboratory came through for us in record time. The DNA for Evenden that was supposed to take three months was done in six weeks. Evenden was eliminated from the semen found on Tanya Smith. DNA results for Evenden on the other cases would take longer.

Along with the elimination DNA results came additional results in relation to the semen found on Tanya Smith and the saliva on the bite-mark. Prior to making the bite-mark comparison, Dr. Sweet had taken a swab of the skin damage by the bite. Remarkably, saliva found in the bite-mark yielded enough DNA material for comparison, and the saliva in the bite-mark was found to be the same DNA profile as the semen. In other words, the person who bit the nipple was the same person who committed the sexual assault. Facts again were supportive of the single-suspect theory.

With this solid DNA profile and the bite-mark now in hand, we had two very solid means for objectively eliminating suspects. The fact that the DNA turnaround time was six weeks and the bite-mark could be done in four days made our preferred method the bite-mark. Moreover, since the DNA confirmed that the biter was depositor of the semen, elimination for one amounted to elimination for the other. This is the kind of physical evidence that investigators can only hope to find. Once a suspect is in custody and charged, this kind of physical evidence is very difficult to dispute in court.

After Evenden's arrest in early December, and as the investigation moved along through December and into mid-February, the partner agencies once again started to posture for the return of their personnel. The trail of the killer and the threats seemed to have grown cold. With no additional phone calls or contacts from him since October 31, 1995, the comments were being made that perhaps he had left the area.

On February 14, 1996, at a meeting with the two main partner agencies, I was once again called upon to justify the use of all of these personnel for the continuation of the investigation. With other serious crimes going uninvestigated, both Chilliwack and Abbotsford made it clear that they were in desperate need for their major crime investigators back. After some debate, it was agreed that the investigation needed to continue; however, downsizing would be revisited in two weeks' time. With thousands of tips still on the books, a time line to consider downsizing in two weeks would mean the investigation would slow to a snail's pace. My protests fell on deaf ears, and I was admonished to consider the bigger picture and greater needs of the partner organizations instead of being too single-minded about this one murder case that might never be solved.

On February 15, 1996, the remaining DNA results came through clearing George Evenden of the other sexual assault for which he had been charged. Evenden was a free man, and the media gathered to update the final chapter on this story of the man wrongly suspected of being the Abbotsford Killer and wrongly charged for the sexual assault of another woman. It was once again front-page news. The man accused as the Abbotsford Killer was now free, and the question was being asked in the media: Where is the Abbotsford Killer?

BACK IN TOUCH

The next communication from the killer came in what was clearly a response to the recent round of media attention about the release of Evenden. Having remained silent for fourteen weeks, since the phone call of October 31, 1995, the next contact came in the most unusual form.

In the early afternoon of February 17, 1996, the disc jockey at the local Abbotsford "Radio Max" radio station received a phone call on the public line. The male caller instructed him to go out to the parking lot and check the Radio Max car. Thinking that someone had perhaps damaged the car, he complied. Upon arriving at the parking lot, he discovered that the headstone from Tanya Smith's grave had been placed onto the hood of the Radio Max vehicle.

Gravestone on Radio Max car

Police arriving at the scene recognized this as another contact from the killer and immediately saturated the area, interviewing everyone found nearby who might be a witness. The parking area behind the radio station is only one block off Abbotsford's main street, South Fraser Way, and the Radio Max parking lot sits adjacent to a restaurant with a full row of windows in open view facing the lot. You would think that someone in a parking lot doing something as unusual as lifting a 190-pound granite headstone out of a vehicle and placing it onto the hood of another car would catch someone's eye. No one in the area saw anything. Our invisible man had struck again; however, he couldn't just leave the headstone without a message. The message was etched in pen across the surface of the headstone around the embossed photograph and across the image of Tanya Smith's face. He scribbled:

- She was not the first she won't be the last
- I'm still looking
- One day Misty
- You won't find me

On either side of an arrow drawn to point at Tanya's right breast, the words "Yummy Tit" were written; once again, clearly a reference to the holdback evidence, confirming that it was our killer.

Defaced gravestone

As the investigative teams gathered again in the task force office and reviewed our new pieces of evidence, several things were clear:

1. Our suspect had not left the area and felt comfortable that he wouldn't be found
2. He was threatening to kill again and was specifically threatening Misty
3. He was intimating that he has killed before and we were perhaps dealing with a serial killer
4. He was going to continue to leave us references to the bite-mark as his signature
5. He had been silent and now clearly seemed to be acting out because of the media attention

Dusting the Radio Max car and the headstone failed to produce any fingerprints. That would have been too good to be true. From his comments in his earlier phone calls, he was obviously careful not to leave prints. But fingerprints are not the only form of evidence we can seek. Whenever someone does something like this, it opens up a variety of opportunities for gathering evidence.

Teams were assigned to follow up at the cemetery where the headstone had been taken, while others were assigned the task of having the handwriting examined.

Investigators met again with the psychological profilers to discuss the theft of the headstone and further explore this person's apparent response to the media. Was there a way that we could exploit this?

This latest strange communication also served to escalate the threat level. The killer had not left the area, and the threat to both Misty and others in the community was still present. The headstone threat, "I'm still looking," coupled with his previous telephone threat, "I'll be cruising around looking for someone else," had to be taken seriously. It was now my turn to go to the partner agencies and talk about personnel. This time the plan would be to escalate the investigation.

The sad task of telling Tanya's family that their daughter's grave had been desecrated had to be faced, and, adding further pain to the process, the gravestone would have to be kept as an exhibit for court. Passing on this latest news just felt like stacking more insult onto the existing injury and expecting the families to cope, and they did somehow manage to cope. Seeing and feeling the pain of the family, team members put forward the idea that the team should replace the headstone. The Abbotsford Police Chief Barry Daniel immediately accepted this idea, and the funds for a new headstone were allocated as an investigational expense. Several of us attended the ceremony to replace the headstone with the Smith family. It was identical to the stone that was taken.

From what I have seen as a police officer over three decades, for people to cope with grief and live through this kind of experience takes an incredible amount of personal strength, family support, and time. These victims all showed incredible strength and had good family support. We all hoped that time would show them some relief of their pain.

The investigation into the theft of the headstone was continuing. As the investigative teams started reporting in on February 18, 1996, it looked like we were going to get a break. The team investigating at the cemetery found that one of the neighbors whose property bordered the entry to the cemetery had seen a suspicious vehicle the night before in the area of Tanya's grave. The entire cemetery is fairly small and flat. Standing anywhere on the grounds, one would be able to survey the entire property.

Arial photo of cemetery

The witness located had taken some time watching the vehicle and was certain that it was an older model Volkswagen van with a custom after-market paint job. This strange paint job, with long palm leaves flowing from the rocker panel over the roof, sounded like it would be easy to find. Our composite artist, Robert Exter, worked with the witness and produced a drawing to depict this vehicle. If it was not the suspect's vehicle, perhaps it was someone who saw the theft of the headstone take place. An immediate media release was developed, asking for the public's assistance in locating the vehicle of interest.

VOLKSWAGEN VAN
Late 1960's to early 1970's light blue Volkswagon van.
Composite drawing of Volkswagen van

The media was only too happy to make the release. Any information in regards to the theft of the headstone was being broadcasted on national news networks.

In light of the most recent events, it was not difficult to get the partner agencies to accept that the level of the investigation needed to be escalated. Every time the suspect made contact, new investigative leads were generated. New opportunities were possible if we had the resources and were prepared to take advantage. I explained that the investigation was now active on four different fronts, each requiring personnel to make it work.

Was the investigative front where we followed up on tips and leads called in through the tips line.

The reactive investigative front where we needed to be ready to respond to the next contact made by the suspect and exploit all possible opportunities that were generated by that contact.

The intelligence front was where we would look at the information that we already had and would try to determine other areas where additional critical information could be gleaned.

The pro-active front where new strategies were generated to gain further information or to get the suspect to expose himself further.

ANOTHER CALL, A NEW WITNESS

It was agreed by the partner agencies that because of the mobility of this suspect and the nature of the threat, there was a need to move our investigation to a provincial project level. On February 19, 1996, as the investigation was once again starting to accelerate, another 911 call was received from the pay phone next to the running track at Rotary Stadium only two blocks from the police office:

Operator: 911 emergency. Do you need police, fire of ambulance?
Caller: How did you like the present I gave you guys? Huh?
Operator: I'm sorry sir. I can't hear you sir.
Call: How did you like the present I gave you guys?
Operator: I'm sorry I can't.
Caller: It won't be the last.

By now, completely attuned to this kind of call response,

the dispatch center had eight patrol cars heading for Rotary Stadium immediately. This time there would be a break. A young woman jogging on the track noticed a man in his late twenties, early thirties on the pay phone. She also saw an older-model beige vehicle parked near the gate into the jogging area. After getting off the phone, she recalled that the man came and stood for a moment with his arms crossed, looking at the track. Although she did not see him get into the vehicle, she was certain when she next looked up that the man was gone and the vehicle was pulling away. The vehicle was described as an older-model two-tone beige and brown sedan. This new description fit with the description of the vehicle seen on the night of the October thirty-first phone call at Gigi's Sports Bar.

Those of us working on the case only had to hear the voice once to know it was the same as heard on the other calls. The question, "How do you like the present I gave you guys?" was an obvious reference to the headstone theft that had occurred two days earlier. The difference in this communication was that he had not used his usual reference to the bite-mark to identify himself. The media were immediately alerted to the call on their scanners and arrived at the police office, anxious for fresh news. This time we decided, because he had not used his holdback verification, we would only confirm that we had received another telephone call but would not confirm that it was from the killer.

Our witness at the Rotary Stadium did not see the caller's face well enough to describe him, but she could give a general description of his stature and build. She estimated that he was around thirty years of age, six feet tall, with an athletic build and reddish-brown hair.

Misty worked with Exter again and provided a drawing that gave her impression of stature for the attacker. The end result showed a man of medium build dressed in everyday casual blue jeans and tee shirt garb similar to dozens of men one might see on any day walking the streets of Abbotsford.

Exter's drawing of the vehicle that emerged from the Rotary Stadium witness was similarly nondescript: an older-model full-sized sedan that was two-tone beige in color.

AMERICAN MODEL SEDAN
Later 1970's to early 1980's American Model Sedan

Composite drawing of Rotary Stadium suspect vehicle

People sometimes comment that creating and releasing these kind of vague images is futile. They seem to lack enough specific directive information to make them worthwhile. What do we hope to accomplish?

Experience has taught us that one really needs to be careful not to focus the mind of the public on some specifics that might be used as eliminators. It is better to give information in the broadest focus and allow the public to make their own links between the variety of facts available.

THE LETTER

Only two days after the Rotary Stadium phone call, the killer came up with yet another way to communicate to police. At 10:30 p.m. on February 21, 1996, on a dark, deserted residential side street, he walked up to the front of a house and threw an object through the living room's plate-glass window. The resident of the house, a young mother home alone with her children, immediately called police.

This was a strange new twist on communications. Officers arriving on the scene were met by a very frightened young woman who pointed them to an object on the living room floor.

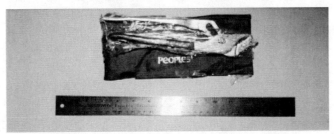

Wrench and envelope thrown through window

The object consisted of a dark blue envelope Scotch-taped to an adjustable metal wrench. Instructions were printed on both sides of the envelope with large block letters in black felt pen.

From the Abby Killer
Call 911

Envelope addressed to call police

A half-dozen uniformed officers canvassed the neighborhood for witnesses to the latest event. The all-too-familiar "no one saw anything" was again our net return for the new surfacing of the killer. The envelope itself would prove to be more fruitful.

Officers carefully placed the envelope and wrench into an evidence bag and transported it to the police office. Abbotsford Police Forensic Identification expert Constable Mike Olsen received the exhibit and started the painstaking procedure of examining the entire package for prints. Each layer was examined as he carefully separated the wrench from the envelope and the tape.

Taking great care as he unraveled the tape, Mike was able to dust the sticky side of the tape for prints, and to everyone's delight, he found a fingerprint. Usually, when a print is found, it is only a partial impression, and in these partial impressions there are generally insufficient characteristics to enable a search to be made. But this was an almost full-fingertip impression. The print he found was so large that it showed almost all of the searchable surfaces of a full-finger impression, and it would be searchable through the national fingerprint database.

If the person who left the print had a criminal record, he or she would definitely be identified with this search. Getting the search done was an immediate priority.

As the rest of the envelope was disassembled, more surprises emerged. The envelope contained four newspaper clippings and a letter, apparently for the police.

Two of the newspaper clippings were pictures of Misty and Tanya that had been released to the media as part of the investigation. Across Misty's forehead, the words "Lucky to be alive" were printed. The third and fourth clippings were articles relating to the deaths of three women who were the victims of sexually motivated murders in 1985. All three of these unsolved murders had been the subject of *Vancouver Sun* newspaper articles back in 1989, and these clipping came from one of those 1989 papers. Someone had been hanging onto these clippings for a very long time. These cases would become the subject of review and follow-up to determine if there was any related evidence that might be linked to our crime. Finally, the letter in the envelope to the police made reference to the newspaper articles and claimed credit for other attacks on women in Abbotsford. Typed in almost all lowercase font, the letter was structured in point form. The following is a replica of the letter:

hello, it's me!!!

yes sir re, tanya's right nipple sure did taste good.

by the way tanya was wearing sandals that night and i threw them with her other stuff

she wasn't a bad lay either.

it was me that phoned from the rotary that night.

you cops getting a little pissed off yet.

hard to catch someone who is smart, not like some stupid crooks

that are no minds.

here are a few more of my conquests. i told you it wasn't my first.

it won't be my last either: i don't stay with the same MO. i have done more after these

ones also. go figure out which ones look in b.c., alta, and a few in Washington state.

how come you guys haven't clued into some of the incidents here in town the last

couple of years.

RE: bourquin cr. by mcDonalds, teen who was attempted sex assault i grabbed

her breasts and was about to gag her when she took off on me.

oriole dr. i almost had that woman beat senseless and was about to rape

her when a car came along. i sure don't need to be
seen.

how about right across from the hospital. hey,,
that was the same bat that was used on misty and
tanya.

as soon as i saw it was an Indian i said no way, could
have aids.

so i took her backpack found $200 in it and threw it
atop the old brick stored

HEY GUYS I'M BAD

I WILL STRIKE AGAIN ONE DAY

I WILL NOT BE CAUGHT

I WILL NOT MOVE FROM ABBOTSFORD

Bye guys this is the last time you here
from me till next time.

GOOD LUCK!!

As we started to break the letter down, it was clear that this
communication was from the killer. Cryptic as it was, he had
managed to pack a huge amount of information into just one
page. Before we started to look at the message content, the
addressing on the envelope spoke volumes.

FROM THE ABBY KILLER
Call 911

Apparent from this address, he had decided to take on the
name that the media dubbed him. The Abby Killer or the
Abbotsford Killer had clearly become a famous—or infamous—person. Apparently, he liked that title. As we pro-

ceeded through the letter itself, the text was examined for additional facts, meaning, and intent.

> **hello, it's me!!!**
> **yes sir re, tanya's right nipple sure did taste good.**

A remarkably friendly/cocky salutation followed by the holdback bite-mark reference, his usual means of verifying that this was a genuine communications.

> **by the way tanya was wearing sandals that night**
> **and i threw them with her other stuff**

Again, more holdback evidence that only he and the police were aware of. Misty had given Tanya sandals to wear when they had left the house. We had mistakenly told the media that we were looking for Tanya's Docker brand shoes.

> **she wasn't a bad lay either.**

Was this comment just disgusting rhetoric to show how lightly he took his actions? Or perhaps he knew that being so flippant toward his victim would infuriate police.

> **it was me that phoned from the rotary that night.**

Because he did not use the verification of the bite-mark, we would not give him media credit that this was his phone call. He wanted to make sure that we knew it was him.

> **you cops getting a little pissed off yet.**

> **hard to catch someone who is smart, not like some**
> **stupid crooks**
> **that are no minds.**

This seemed to demonstrate that he thought what he was doing was really a game against the police and that he was smarter than the average player. His comments about criminals actually show some disdain for dumb crooks and illustrate his feeling of superiority.

> **here are a few more of my conquests. i told you it**
> **wasn't my first. .**

The fact that he refers to his attacks on women as conquests may be the reflection of power and control. The attack is more about power and control than it is about sex. The violent sexual assault and murder becomes a personal victory. The victim is objectified as something he has conquered or overcome.

> **it won't be my last either: i don't stay with the same**
> **MO. i have done more after these ones also. Go**
> **figure out which ones look in b.c., alta, and a few in**
> **Washington state.**

Reading this and seeing an apparent reference to the enclosed newspaper articles about the 1985 murders, we began to suspect that we may in fact be dealing with a real serial killer. The two murder articles from the 1989 newspaper had been saved somewhere for six years. Was this a killer who could perpetrate horrific, violent murders ten years ago and then literally become dormant until the need for another spree?

Or was he elsewhere, terrorizing other communities? The Green River investigation, still ongoing, came to mind. Whoever he was, he had sufficient knowledge of police work to understand that the police looked at criminal incidents searching for similar Modus Operandi (MO) to link incident to incident or sometimes incidents to perpetrators with an identifiable history for a particular criminal act.

> how come you guys haven't clued into some of the incidents here in town the last
> couple of years.
> RE: bourquin cr. by mcDonalds, teen who was attempted sex assault i grabbed
> her breasts and was about to gag her when she took off on me.
> oriole dr. i almost had that woman beat senseless and was about to rape
> her when a car came along. i sure don't need to be seen.
> how about right across from the hospital. hey,, that was the same bat that was used on misty and tanya.
> as soon as i saw it was an Indian i said no way, could have aids.

This statement was easy to verify. All three of these incidents were unsolved attacks on women. All three files were pulled and scanned for additional evidence that might help us identify our suspect.

HEY GUYS I'M BAD
I WILL STRIKE AGAIN ONE DAY

I WILL NOT BE CAUGHT
I WILL NOT MOVE FROM ABBOTSFORD
            Bye guys this is the last time you here
from me till next time.
                    GOOD LUCK!!

The meanings of these final comments are somewhat self-evident; however, they do reflect an arrogant, threatening tone, along with an almost friendly adversarial challenge.

Was there a way that we could capitalize on this man's need to play a game with the police and his apparent appreciation and reaction to media attention?

The investigative team was going full out chasing down tips and eliminating possible suspects. This latest letter only served to escalate things even further.

NEW CASES, NEW OPPORTUNITIES, NEW EVIDENCE

Special tip-assignment teams were formed to follow up on the three attacks on Abbotsford women identified in the letter. Forensic Identification members were moving to search the print from the tape against the Canadian Criminal database. Investigators were contacted from the three unsolved homicides identified in the newspaper clippings. Were there any similarities? Were there any common suspects, names, or persons of interest common to our case anywhere in their investigations?

Once again we called upon our psychological profiling team from Ottawa to review the facts and give their advice. Only this time the advice would not be to determine a criminal profile, but rather to assist in developing strategies to encourage the killer to expose himself to be apprehended.

Inspector Ron McKay and his team of profilers attended,

and as they arrived, we were able to provide them with a wide range of new information.

The content of the letter was truly significant. As investigators returned with results of their inquiries on the three Abbotsford assaults, the attacks described were confirmed as real incidents:

> **RE: bourquin cr. by mcDonalds, teen who was attempted sex assault i grabbed**
> **her breasts and was about to gag her when she took off on me.**

This sentence related to an incident that occurred at 10:05 p.m. on July 5, 1995, a twelve-year-old girl was sitting on the front lawn of a building on the busy street across from McDonald's when a male came up from behind her and grabbed her breast. He put his hand over her mouth and attempted to drag her away. She fought her way free and ran. Although she did not see the suspect's face, she described his arms as being freckled and covered with reddish hair. When he had his arm around her neck, she saw a distinctive tattoo of an anchor on his right forearm.

The girl worked with Exter and produced a drawing of a naval insignia commonly known as a "fouled anchor." This looks like a typical double hook and shank anchor with the chain wrapped around the shank.

Composite drawing of anchor tattoo

The next offence on Oriole Drive had happened on September 16, 1994, at 10:30 p.m.

> **oriole dr. i azlmost had that woman beat senseless and was about to rape**
> **her when a car came along. i sure don't need to be seen.**

In this case, a woman living in an outpatient home for persons with mental illness had gone out for an evening walk. It was very dark, and the victim remembered being struck from behind on the head. She regained consciousness while being dragged by her feet. The suspect let go of her and fled when a car came down the street.

The most interesting incident was the most recent event reference in the letter.

> **how about right across from the hospital. hey,, that was the same bat that was used on misty and tanya. as soon as i saw it was an Indian i said no way, could have aids.**
> **so i took her backpack found $200 in it and threw it atop the old brick stored**

At 5:30 a.m., August 8, 1995, only sixty-seven days prior to the attack on Misty and Tanya, this incident happened on the street across from the front entry of the MSA hospital. Significant to this location, the attack on Misty and Tanya happen almost directly behind the MSA hospital. The distance between crime scene, only three city blocks.

A young woman had left the downtown bar area after having an argument with her boyfriend. Walking past the front of the MSA hospital at around 5:30 a.m. was the last thing this victim remembered. She was found unconscious by a passing motorist lying on the sidewalk and bleeding from the head. Doctors treating her injuries stated that she had a compressed skull fracture caused by blunt-force trauma to the head. With this kind of skull fracture, the bone is actually driven into the brain tissue. The injuries would likely have been fatal without immediate medical intervention. The woman was of eastern European heritage; however, she had a dark complexion and features that could be mistaken for native Indian. Her purse was missing at the time she was found and had only recently been located by a maintenance person on top of a brick retail store to the north of the hospital. Upon regaining consciousness, she confirmed that she had $225.00 cash in her purse that night. Suffering from brain injuries from the blow to her head, the woman still had problems walking and talking when investigators re-interviewed her. The investigation of the case had certainly been a mystery at the time it had happened. Without witnesses or other physical evidence, many possibilities were being considered.

Had this been an attack by the boyfriend that she had the argument with? Investigators had eliminated that possibility.

Was it a robbery? After all, her purse was missing. Was it some kind of random attack? Investigators even wondered if she had perhaps stumbled off the sidewalk and been struck in the head by the mirror of a passing truck.

All of these theories existed as competing scenarios on this file until the letter claiming credit was received. In this case, the knowledge of the location of the discarded purse amounted to holdback information similar to the bite-mark. Only a person with intimate knowledge of what had happened that night would know the location of the discarded purse.

Meetings with investigators from agencies representing the three historical homicides reported in the 1989 newspaper articles produced less-concrete results. Notably, all three of these killings were similar in that they were believed to be sexually motivated. All had evidence of extreme and excessive violence. All appeared to be opportunistic in nature. In other words, the victims were going about their regular business and ended up in the wrong place at the wrong time.

In all three cases purses were taken. There were no known connections between the three cases and no outstanding suspects of interest. No contacts had been made with the police with the possible exception that in one of the cases there was a suspicious phone call made to the victim's family by a male person claiming to be a police officer. The call was investigated at the time and was believed to be a cruel prank.

On February 22, 1996, the print found on the envelope tape was searched through the Canadian fingerprint database in Ottawa and came back negative for positive identification.

How could that be? We were sure almost certain that we were dealing with an experienced criminal. Even the profilers were certain that he would have some kind of criminal past. We needed to search the US fingerprint database. After all, Abbotsford was right on the US boarder with Sumas, Washington, and the letter said that some of his conquests were in Washington State. Maybe he was an American.

Along with the US search, just to be on the safe side, we had a special search done of the Canadian print database, and on February 24, 1996, the results were in again. No match. There was no criminal record of the print in the Canadian or US criminal record databases.

In police investigations, outcomes are never certain. Sometimes you expect results and don't get them, and other times you get results you are not expecting. In sharp contrast to our fingerprint coming up blank, we were receiving literally hundreds of tips on Volkswagen vans with strange paint jobs. A popular mode of transport and shelter for the flower children of the 1970s, many of the vehicles identified in tips were still with their original owners. In the final analysis, we never found the strange vehicle from the cemetery that night. In the end it would turn out to have no connection to the investigation. It was truly one of the many red herring clues that we would chase to the point of exhaustion without productive results. From our tips, we had the most comprehensive list of repainted Volkswagen vans and middle-aged flower children that will ever exist in western Canada.

Certainly chasing down dead-end tips like the Volkswagen van had an effect on the course of the investigation inasmuch as it required hundreds of hours of unproductive investigation.

In contrast to the Volkswagen or any other tip, nothing had a more dramatic effect on our investigative mind-set than the print that could not be matched to a known criminal. If the print had been matched and had identified the suspect, our investigation would have immediately focused on that individual.

Now, instead of becoming more focused, we needed to change our entire way of thinking. This killer, without a criminal history, turned our investigation upside down. We had to start re-examining some of our basic assumptions and strategies. Up to now, priority had been given to looking first at known criminals. Now, in complete contradiction to that thinking, the person responsible for this terrible crime was someone without a criminal record.

Now, for the investigators looking for the Abbotsford Killer, having a criminal record was going to eliminate suspects. What kind of person would this man without a criminal record be? And how do you find a person appearing to be normal in the community, living in relative anonymity?

If we were to take his recent letter and attachments at

face value, we were looking for an experienced serial killer who had not yet been touched by the legal system. Maybe he was as smart as he seemed to think he was.

Where do you look for someone lurking as an opportunistic predator and emerging only long enough to satisfy his needs for violent sex or, now, media attention? How do you find someone hidden in plain view? It was time for more strategies, new strategies.

As we reevaluated our position, it was clear that additional action needed to be taken if we were going to have a chance of apprehending the suspect.

Our tip priority system needed to be reevaluated. Serendipitously, most of the tips that we were actively investigating related to persons with criminal records, and with the new information in hand, the elimination of these tips moved quickly.

OPERATION MOUSETRAP

Media releases continued to encourage the public to call in and listen to the voice tapes. The composite drawing done by Exter was becoming an icon of this investigation. The composite remained on display, and tips continued to be called in on lookalikes.

Likely our most radical undertaking, a new media strategy was developed. The media strategy would be a ploy to challenge the killer to continue to make contact with the police, thus increasing his chances of being apprehended. This strategy needed to be carefully developed and executed. Psychological profilers working on the case warned that saying the wrong thing could have the effect of insulting and enraging the killer, causing him to kill again to prove the point that his threats were not idle. He was responding to the media, and if we were going to say things to provoke a call or a contact, we needed to make sure that the media did not change it or editorialize in any way that would cause a fatal reaction.

For this strategy to work, the media needed to be convinced to cooperate with a most unorthodox undertaking. Media agencies would be asked to participate in an investigative ploy. Using the media for purposes other than sharing information with the public or asking for public assistance is not something police often consider. Anyone familiar with the media will understand what a huge step it is for them to participate in printing or broadcasting anything that is being done in a covert manner. Media ethics dictate a high standard of accountability to the public, and printing anything while knowing it to be a manipulation of the facts is not something that they take lightly.

Fortunately, for our investigation in this case, media agencies were acutely aware of the serious ongoing threat to the community they served. They willingly accepted the need for their assistance in creating a tactical advantage for the police in this case. Constable Elly Sawchuk made the approach to media outlets and gained agreement to the plan. With this agreement in place, media agencies, both print and broadcast, were on board. It was clear that almost everyone wanted to help, and only one small newspaper made a condition, saying, "We will go along with the plan; however, we reserve the right to be critical if something goes wrong."

With this agreement for media cooperation in hand, psychological profilers moved ahead in developing a script of what could be released. Profilers spent a great deal of time deciding on a person through whom the message should be conveyed.

As the scripting was being done, other investigators were working on Operation Mousetrap. Mousetrap was the capture side of the media strategy. This would be a plan to catch the killer while in the process of making a phone call to police.

The most contacts from the killer had come through 911 calls made from pay telephones in the City of Abbotsford.

In this plan, all of the pay telephones in Abbotsford were identified and placed on a geographic grid. The game plan was simple: After the media release was made, police vehicles would be staked out at strategic geographic locations throughout the city, ready to respond to any 911 call from phone booths closest to their location.

All of the phone calls from the killer had been of relatively short time duration—meaning nothing over twenty seconds. It was important that police officers responding to the calls have a better time advantage. With call durations of only twenty seconds, we needed to develop a tactical advantage. If we were going to have any chance of catching this guy at a phone booth, responding officers needed to be on their way to the call before the call was answered by the 911 operator.

The problem was posed to B.C. Tel, the telephone service provider. The initial response was that it couldn't be done; however, knowing the seriousness of the request and after some further deliberation, a group of technicians and engineers put their heads together and called back with a proposal. Ultimately, they designed a system that allowed a special dispatch console in the Abbotsford Police Dispatch Center to display the location of all incoming 911 calls originating at telephone booths. A phone booth 911 call would appear on a viewing screen before the dispatcher picked it up to answer. By allowing the incoming call to ring five times before answering, a twenty-second advantage was gained. The Operation Mousetrap dispatcher viewing the special console would send a car to the location of the phone booth while the 911 operator would answer and talk to the caller.

On March 26, 1996, Operation Mousetrap was launched. Dr. Mike Webster was chosen by the profiling team as the best person to make the statement to the media. Being a local psychologist, Dr. Webster had been quoted in the paper in the past on this case and others. He was credible, and it would not be at all strange for these comments to come from him. A news release was made advising that the investigation was being scaled back because the suspect had not been heard from for and extended period of time.

"He has not been heard from since February 21 and police psychologist Mike Webster Mike Webster commented to the media Monday that he thinks it will be some time before the killer contacts police again

"I think that when he takes these long periods of time off without making contact, these are the times when he's working up the courage or the confidence to make contact again.

"The killer is struggling with two powerful needs—one is the need to demonstrate his power and control over the police and the other to preserve his own freedom.

"I think he understands the risk he takes, and I don't think he feels confident in taking that risk. And looking at the elements of this case, I don't think that he is able over the long period of time to taunt the police like that and not compromise his freedom, his liberty. And I think, at some level, he knows that as well."

With this media release, Operation Mousetrap was set, and the surveillance continued in place with twenty surveillance units placed in strategic location throughout the city for five days. At the end of five days there were no calls from the killer, and the surveillance was terminated; however, the strategy was not abandoned. The surveillance teams had become expert at responding to three or four legitimate 911 pay phone calls per day. They were able to reach most calls in under sixty seconds. If we could come up with another release to bait the killer to call, we would set up and run the mousetrap again.

THE GEOGRAPHIC PROFILE

In spite of the obvious size and personnel commitment, Operation Mousetrap was not the only strategy underway during these new strategy weeks.

Inspector Kim Rossmo was actively working on geographic profiling, and the area-location profile was nearing completion. As mentioned before, geographic profiling looks at the known crime locations of a suspect and from that is able to predict the area where the suspect is most likely to live or work.

In this investigation, we were now working with locations from:

- The attack site
- The body dumpsite
- Four telephone call sites
- The dumpsite of the headstone
- The location where the wrench was thrown through the window

The locations of the three attacks described in the letter Inspector Rossmo had eleven sites to work into his formula. From this he was able to produce an overlay map depicting a twenty square-block area of Abbotsford City, and he provided the areas where the killer would most likely live.

It was the intent of the investigative team to use this information to assist in prioritizing tips as well as being part of a comprehensive data search.

In addition to geographic profiling, an enhanced crime poster depicting new information was prepared for release. The new poster included a sketch of the Rotary Stadium suspect vehicle, the VW van from the cemetery, the suspect composite drawing, the stature drawing, as well as a drawing of the anchor tattoo described by the teenage victim from the McDonald's attack. This poster was intended to provide the public with a comprehensive overview of case-related information, enabling them to make links between their own knowledge and case-related facts.

The plan was for the release of this new comprehensive-information poster to the media, along with an enhanced version of the voice tapes. One of our team members, Constable Peter Jadis, had taken the initiative to have the tapes cleaned by a professional sound lab to remove static and white noise.

On April 30, 1996, a media conference was called. The intent of the conference was:

- To release the new information poster
- To refocus the public attention on the voice tapes
- To offer a reward of forty thousand dollars.

• This reward had been accumulated over the past five months: ten thousand from the City of Abbotsford, ten thousand from the City of Chilliwack, and twenty thousand from two private parties who wished to remain anonymous.

A CALL FROM THE KILLER'S MOTHER

On April 30, 1996, at 10:00 a.m., Constable Elly Sawchuk hosted the media conference at the Abbotsford Police Office. The media response, as usual, was a full house. The enhanced tapes were played, and the comprehensive poster was displayed and explained.

Comprehensive-information poster released to media

Prior to the conference, the new tapes were loaded onto the special call-in line for persons wanting to listen to the tape again. Within an hour of the conference, our new enhanced media strategy was on the air across the Province of British Columbia and beyond.

Only three hours after the conference concluded, at 1:20 p.m. on April 30th, task force Detective Len Georke received a tip call from a distraught woman who told him that she had personally listened to the tapes on the police playback line and she was certain that it was the voice of her son. She explained that although her son did not fit the composite drawing, he drove a vehicle that fit the description of the suspect vehicle, he liked to fish at Vedder River, he lived one block from the Rotary Stadium where the fifth phone call was made, and he had mentioned to family members that he had attended Tanya Smith's funeral. The woman declined to give her name; however, she did provide her son's name as Terry Grant Driver, born January 27, 1965.

At 2:22 p.m., on April 30, Detective Georke received two more calls from the same woman providing further information. Her son owned a police scanner, and on October 28, 1995, at a family gathering, during an argument with his brother, he said, "Don't f*** with me. You don't know me anymore, and you don't know what I am capable of doing."

From the information provided by the caller, it was confirmed that Terry Driver lived in a residential neighborhood only one block north of Rotary Stadium.

This was considered a high-priority tip, and at 4:20 p.m., a nine-person surveillance team, including primary investigators Sergeant Bill Emery and Corporal Kevin MacLeod, set up on Driver's house.

At 5:17 p.m., Driver arrived home in his brown 1982 Pontiac Grand Prix. The vehicle certainly fit the description; however, it was apparent to everyone that Driver's facial features were substantially different. Emery and MacLeod decided that they would utilize the "cold approach" strategy to gather further evidence.

In many cases, when a suspect is identified during normal homicide investigations, lengthy surveillance is conducted to establish lifestyle, movements, and associates. In this investigation, now into its seventh month, new suspects were being identified on a daily basis. We did not have the luxury of committing days of surveillance to every suspect. This cold approach had been used frequently as a means of confronting the suspect with the bad news that someone had identified them as a possible suspect and we were looking for an elimination. After all, we did have a fingerprint, DNA, and a bite-mark impression that we could used for elimination purposes.

In most cold approaches, the identified persons were usually willing and anxious to get their name cleared.

As they approached Terry Driver's door, Emery and MacLeod decided that there would be no point in telling Terry that his own mother had turned him in. If he was eliminated, it would be a terrible wedge to have driven into any family relationship. The approach was: "Someone has identified you as a possible suspect, and we need to speak to you."

Driver's first reaction was non-emotional and measured. Emery and MacLeod could not read this response one way or the other.

During the interview, Driver advised Emery and MacLeod that he had worked at Abbotsford Printing for the last six years. On last Halloween night, the night of the fourth recorded call, he had been out trick-or-treating with his kids from 6:00 p.m. to 8:30 p.m. Unfortunately, both his kids were too young to provide any confirmation of their father's activities. He admitted that he liked to fish at Vedder River. When asked if he would supply fingerprints or DNA samples, Driver declined. The interview was concluded at 6:00 p.m.

As we reviewed the tip follow-up at the office, both Emery and MacLeod were feeling somewhat frustrated. He sounded like the tape, but he certainly didn't look at all like the composite. The tip details from his own mother were also significant, particularly the voice recognition and the information about attending Tanya's funeral.

At 7:20 p.m., April 30, MacLeod called Driver again and asked that he attend for DNA and fingerprints. Driver again declined, advising that he would call back tomorrow.

Around noon the next day, Driver called Bill Emery and told him that he had been told by friends, family, and coworkers to seek legal advice prior to cooperating with the police. He intended to see a well-known local defence lawyer, Mr. G. Jack Harris, but could not get in until May 2, 1996.

As we awaited Driver's contact with his lawyer, the investigation into his personal history continued. Driver's mother was located and spoken to regarding her son. It was learned that other family members had also listened to the phone lines, and the family had agreed together that the call to police needed to be made.

An in-depth examination of Terry Driver's personal history continued. The story emerged of a boy with a troubled and tragic childhood. One of four children, Driver was the son of a retired Vancouver City Police officer. Terry was born with brain damage. He was an unmanageable child, so-much-so that he had to be placed into a special-care facility at age five. While he was in care, his parents divorced. Driver's history in care was troubled and included acts of violence against both persons and animals. At around eleven years of age, Terry moved in with his father, where he stayed until he was eighteen years old. Eventually entering trade school, he pursued a career in printing. Interviews with other family members confirmed the facts and provided additional information. Now married to a wife ten years his senior, he had two small children and had moved with this family to Abbotsford four years earlier.

Interviews with Driver's employer at a local printing firm produced time-sheet records that showed Driver was away from work during the times when the critical phone calls were made on October 18, 1995.

After several more phone calls to Driver to determine if he would attend and supply DNA and fingerprints, finally on May 2, 1996, Corporal MacLeod spoke to G. Jack Harris. Mr. Harris advised that his client would not supply either DNA or fingerprints.

After further contact with family members, it was determined that Driver's family and his boss had been encouraging Terry to go to the police office and provide the information need to confirm he was not the killer.

DO YOU THINK I'D BE STUPID ENOUGH TO LEAVE FINGERPRINTS?

On May 3, 1996, Corporal MacLeod contacted G. Jack Harris once again. On this occasion, Mr. Harris advised that his client had relented and would now provide fingerprints only. There was a condition: He would only provide prints if they were taken in Mr. Harris's presence. If they did not match, they would be destroyed immediately.

On May 3, 1996, at 11:47 a.m., Terry Driver and his lawyer, G. Jack Harris, presented themselves at the front counter of the Abbotsford Police Department. Sergeant Emery, Corporal MacLeod, and I met them there.

Mr. Harris produced a document confirming the conditions under which the fingerprints would be taken. Our meeting adjourned to the cellblock area where we met with forensic identification expert Constable Gerry Ennis. We all stood around the small room as Constable Ennis took Driver's prints. Hardly a word was spoken except by Ennis, who was providing directions to Driver to facilitate the rolling of the prints. Even Jack Harris, who generally had something to say to break an uncomfortable silence, stood mute during the process.

A lawyer will never knowingly bring a client in to submit to an incriminating process unless the client has expressed the desire to come clean and turn himself in. That was certainly not the case here. Jack Harris clearly believed that they would be walking out of the police office together.

Once the prints were completed, I accompanied Constable Ennis across the cellblock area to another glassed-in guard's room that was still in sight of Terry Driver and Jack Harris.

As all experts should, Constable Ennis took his time isolating and counting the points of comparison that could render the print as a positive match. Working back and forth between Driver's known prints and the unknown print from the tape, Ennis used his powerful magnifying glass and two small pointer sticks to count his characteristic matches. After approximately twenty minutes, it was done. Ennis turned to me and said, "It is a match. So far I have counted eleven points of comparison." Ennis added, "When I rolled it, I could see immediately that it was a good possibility because it had the unusual little hockey stick characteristic in the center."

Those were the words I was waiting for, but the impact of actually hearing them seemed too good to be true. A grin from ear to ear would have properly reflected how I felt, but

the appropriate decorum to convey the message that someone is being arrested for murder did not allow for anything
but a somber poker face.

I quietly congratulated Gerry Ennis and thanked him.
I could see Bill Emery looking at me from the room where
they all stood waiting. As I left the room where the comparison was made, Bill was the only one looking my way for
a moment, and I gave him an affirmative nod. He turned his
head sideways, as if not knowing how to interpret my signal.
It would soon be clear. Immediately upon entering the room,
I spoke directly to Mr. Harris. "Mr. Harris, your client's print
is a match. I turned to Bill and motioned towards Driver
saying, "Sergeant Emery, arrest that man."

Both Emery and MacLeod remained stoic and com-
posed as Sergeant Emery placed Terry Driver under arrest
for the murder of Tanya Smith and the attempted murder
of Misty Cockerill.

Driver sat and accepted the results without reaction.
Clearly, at least some part of him knew this might happen, and he was ready for the possibility. Mr. Harris, on the
other hand, was clearly shocked and needed a moment to
fully consider the implications of what had just happened.
A skilled defence counsel and advocate for his clients, Mr.
Harris had taken his client at his word.

In spite of the fact that Mr. Harris had objected on his
client's behalf and claimed duress, he had also agreed to allow
his client to participate in the fingerprinting process. Duress
claims or not, Driver clearly had the benefit of counsel and
had chosen to partake in the process voluntarily.

Terry Driver was taking a calculated risk that Mr. Harris

didn't know about. Terry Driver, who asked in one of his phone calls, "Do you think I would be stupid enough to leave fingerprints behind when I make a phone call?" was apparently confident enough that he hadn't left prints anywhere. He was going to take his chance to get the police off his back. Mr. Harris left the cellblock area and stated that he would contact another defence counsel to represent Driver. If we did our jobs right, and if the justice system worked, these would be the first moments of the first day of Terry Driver's life in prison. Terry Driver would not leave the secure custody of prison walls.

LIFTING THE WEIGHT OF THE WORLD

After the booking was competed, I met with Bill and Kevin in the task force office. As we shook hands, the propriety and solemn decorum was dispelled and smiles emerged. It was time to bring in the team and let everyone know that our killer was in custody.

An emergency pager message was sent out to all of the investigators on duty, requesting that they return to the office. As detectives returned in teams of two, they were told of the positive identification.

Our bad guy was in custody, and the massive manhunt was over. As the good news was conveyed, we witnessed the full range of responses from high-fives and hoots of delight to somber faces and tear-filled eyes. An enormous weight was lifted off everyone's shoulders. The immediate threat of a killer lurking in our community was over. It would have been nice to pause and dwell longer in those moments, savoring relief and accomplishment, but we all knew that we didn't have the luxury of time. We needed to move quickly to obtain and execute search warrants on Driver's home, vehicle, and workplace. With Driver in custody, the warrants for dental impressions and DNA samples could wait a few days, but the other evidence needed to be secured as soon as possible.

With warrants in hand, teams of investigators were dispatched to secure the Driver residence to search his home and vehicle for anything that might further connect him to the case. In particular, we were looking for a police scanner, the computer, and printer used to construct the note, as well as footwear that might match impressions found at the river near the drag marks. Any additional newspaper clippings or anything with bloodstains would also be of great interest.

Driver's car was seized from the family garage, along with his wife's small car. Both were transported by flat-deck truck to the police office, where they would be carefully examined for fingerprints, bloodstains, as well as hair and fibers.

Driver's crime vehicle

Although we were confident that Driver would be a positive match to the DNA and the bite-mark, we had no intention of leaving additional stones unturned. If there was more evidence, we were going to find it. A warrant was executed at Driver's place of work to look for attendance records as well as any related evidence that he may have kept there.

As these searches progressed, we intentionally had not yet notified the victims' families that we had a suspect in custody. A team of investigators with a photo lineup of Driver would present it to Misty before she could become aware that we had made an arrest. We did not want to face any arguments in court that we had prejudiced the lineup by making the victim aware of the arrest in advance. This would be just one of dozens of photo lineups that Misty had already seen. As it turned out, Misty was not able to pick Driver out of the photo lineup. This was not really a surprise considering the nature of the offence, the speed and violence of the attack, and the subsequent head injury she had sustained. It was not really an issue if all the other physical evidence connecting Driver to the attack came through.

Notwithstanding the negative photo lineup, this was a great day for Misty and her family. After seven months in police protection and living in hiding, they were finally able to feel the relief of knowing the threat was over. They could return to their home, and the kids could go back to school.

The Smith family was also contacted and notified that an arrest had been made. Both families needed to be certain that we had the right person. After seven months, it was hard for them to believe that it was finally over and the threat had ended. Eventually there would be a court case to contend with, but that was a long way down the road.

After searching Driver's house, very little new evidence turned up: the police scanner, which was set up and programmed to include Abbotsford Police and Chilliwack RCMP frequencies, a couple of pairs of boots of which the tread marks would not be a match, a computer and printer, which were consistent with the production of the note but not conclusively identifiable, and, interestingly, a baseball cap with the Sea Scout insignia.

The Sea Scout insignia, a "fouled anchor," was a close match to the anchor described by the twelve-year-old victim of the attempted abduction across from the McDonald's.

Notably, Misty had also mentioned that she thought she saw a tattoo on her attacker's arm; however, the tattoo she described was a butterfly.

Surprisingly, Driver had no tattoos on his arms. This led us to speculate that, with his knowledge of police work from his father, he may have been drawing tattoos on his own arms as distracters or false clues to aid in evading identification and capture.

The search of Driver's car was another protracted and thorough task undertaken by the forensic identification specialists. Considering that the body of the victim was transported in the car, there was a possibility of a two-way transfer of materials. Blood, fingerprints, hair, and fibers from the victim or her clothing might still be in the vehicle, and fiber from the trunk of the car might be on the victim or her discarded clothing. In examining the trunk, the car's trunk-liner carpet was missing, and residual fibers of the liner were collected from the floor of the trunk. This great effort in examination would pay off. A fiber found during the autopsy on Tanya's eyebrow would ultimately be found to match to fibers found on the floor of the trunk.

As the day ended, exhibits were marked and put away. Notes were completed and plans were made to proceed with the dental and DNA warrants as soon as possible. Team members who had finished their tasks hours before stayed until everyone was done. The bond that had grown between the members of the task force over those seven months was vividly apparent in the collective need to stay and finish that day in particular together. With the day's work completed, and yet unwilling to separate, the team gathered at a local bar to share a beer and celebrate the hard-won achievement. This wasn't the first time we had taken to go for a beer together, but it was the first time since the start of the investigation that the constraints of frustration and uncertainty were gone. The weight was lifted, and that was evident in the tired but satisfied faces of the team.

It didn't take the media long to figure out that something was up. A media release was carefully drafted. The public needed to know, and had a right to know, that the threat to the community was over and that the police were confident that they had the right person in custody. In delicate balance to this, we could not release information or evidence-related facts that could later be pointed to by a defence counsel as prejudicing the accused person's right to a fair trial. On the morning of May 4, 1996, the media release would identify Terry Grant Driver of Abbotsford British Columbia as the man now charged with the murder of Tanya Smith and the attempted murder of Misty Cockerill.

The release caused another media frenzy as investigative reporters found their own sources on Terry Driver. Media proceeded to interview neighbors and coworkers who all shook their heads in disbelief that Driver could possibly be the Abbotsford Killer.

After the press release, the investigation pressed on. DNA and dental-impression warrants were executed, and samples were obtained from Driver.

Driver's close friend and fishing buddy, Cliff, was identified and interviewed. Cliff confirmed that he and Driver had frequently fished on the Vedder River in the area where the body of Tanya Smith had been found. In fact, on the morning that Smith's body was found, Terry Driver had phoned Cliff from his cell phone, telling him that he was out on the dyke at the Vedder Canal watching the police processing a crime scene. Cliff was aware of the ongoing police investigation and had heard the tapes played through the media. He thought the voice sounded like Driver and, on one occasion, told Driver that he sounded like the voice heard on the tape. Driver denied that this was his voice, and Cliff accepted his denial.

As more information emerged, Driver's cellular telephone became a point of interest. Information was received that Driver carried the cell phone almost all the time, and he would go out at night and do what he described as "scanner chasing." For Driver, "scanner chasing" meant driving around the community, listening to his police scanner, and following police to calls. A check of his scanner records showed that he had made one of his scanner-chasing calls to the police 911 dispatch center on the night of October 13, 1995, just around midnight. In this call Driver reported seeing a man on what he believed to be a stolen bicycle entering an apartment building. A uniformed police officer met Driver outside the building and took his information. The location where this happened was only about eight city blocks from the location where Tanya and Misty would be confronted and attacked some twenty minutes later.

Tracking of these cell phone records also put Driver in the area of the cemetery when the headstone was stolen and in the area of the Vedder Canal on the morning of October 14, 1995, when the body was discovered. In addition to the phone call made to Cliff from the Vedder River that morning, records also showed cell phone calls made to two local media outlets. Both outlets confirmed receiving calls that morning from a male reporting that the police had found a body at Vedder River. Warrants were obtained, and all of Driver's cell phone records were seized as evidence.

As we delved further into our own investigative file, we discovered that Driver had already been touched by the investigation on two occasions. The first was a tip called in on October 18, around eleven p.m. in the evening. This was the same day that the first threatening phone calls were received from the suspect. Still at the office finishing off my notes for the day, I answered the call. The male caller said that a male named Terry who lived in the Trethewey Gardens townhouses with his wife and children had been observed by the paper-delivery girl standing at his front-room window masturbating. The caller thought he could be a person of interest to our investigation. There was no other information on the call to link it to the victims or the crime scene, and consequently it was given a lower priority and was misplaced in the files.

The second link to the existing file was found in the records of Tanya Smith's funeral. Investigators following up on information from Driver's mother that he attended Tanya's funeral reviewed license plate numbers gathered from the parking lot of the church. Driver's plate was found among them. The videotape of mourners coming and going from the funeral was also reviewed. A short segment of the videotape showed Driver, carrying one of his children and holding the other by the hand, leaving the back of the church.

Over the next few weeks, results started being returned from exhibits sent for analysis.

Dr. David Sweet was the first to report back. The dental impressions taken from Driver were characterized as a "probable match" to the bite-mark found on Smith's right nipple. In the science of bite-mark comparison, the possible outcomes from a bite-mark analysis are:

1. Positive identification: there are sufficient characteristics present to establish that the bite-mark is an identical match to the dental impression taken from the suspect.

2. Probable identification: there are some identifiable characteristics present, however insufficient to make a qualified positive match. The suspect is a probable match.

3. Elimination: there are characteristics present in the bite-mark that are inconsistent with the dental impression taken. Then suspect is not the person responsible—elimination.

Under the circumstances, a probable match was an accept-able outcome, and we were still awaiting DNA. Identifiable DNA profiles had been found in both saliva from the bite-mark and semen on Smith's body. These two DNA profiles had already been confirmed as a match to each other back in January. In other words, the person who made the bite-mark had also deposited the semen.

When the results finally came through on the DNA match of Terry Driver to the profiles on Smith's body, it was extremely conclusive. DNA samples showed that Driver was a positive match within a probability of 1 to 1.7 trillion. With these kind of numbers, the court would accept, without a doubt, Driver was the person responsible for the semen and the bite-mark found on Tanya Smith's body.

CASE SOLVED: THE JOURNEY TO TRIAL BEGINS

Now, with our case solved and the bad guy behind bars, the investigative team was able to scale down in size. The priority changed to preparing for the court case to come. Typical of any major homicide case, the accused is permitted by Legal Aid to select a competent defence lawyer. Driver employed the services of Mr. Glen Orris QC, a well-known Vancouver lawyer often found at the defence bench in high-profile murder trials.

The Senior Regional Crown Counsel Sean Madigan was assigned to prosecute the case. The murder trial we were facing would require both skill and experience, and Madigan was one of the most senior of the Regional Crown Prosecutors. He had an extensive history as a prosecutor of murder cases. Mr. Madigan's junior partner on the case was Neil MacKenzie. Neil, a former Abbotsford Crown

Prosecutor, was well known to most of us and would provide more of the sense of team that we needed as we prepared with prosecution for the trial.

Most people who are not involved in the process of criminal investigations have no idea how much time and effort are required to get a homicide case ready to go to court. All exhibits must be established in a chain of continuity from the moment they are seized by police to the time they are placed before the judge. Witnesses must be interviewed by prosecutors to prepare for the trial process. Every statement of fact and every exhibit that is intended to be submitted to the court to form part of the evidence must be traced to its roots and verified. Is it truly a fact, and can it be proven in court? All evidence that the police and Crown have in relation to the case must be shared with the defence prior to the trial in a process known as "disclosure."

This disclosure process is intended to provide the accused with the full benefit of all available information to enable the building of a defence case. The process is labor intensive for police and crown. In this particular case, it involved the defence attending at the Abbotsford Police office for almost two weeks, reviewing all of the available evidence from any of the 9,400 tips in any file they chose to see.

As the trial approached, Glen Orris advised Crown by letter that he was made aware that there might be an alternate suspect that the police were not aware of.

In response to this letter, Sergeant Emery and I attended to the office of Mr. Orris to investigate the possibility. In our meeting with Mr. Orris, he advised that there was another male subject seen that night in the area of the attack site. Dressed in dark clothing, the alternate subject was seen emerging from the hedge area where the girls had been attacked and was noted as running north across Bevan Avenue. Mr. Orris admitted that this version of events was coming from his client, Terry Driver. When we asked if we could interview Driver in person in relation to the accounting of events, Mr. Orris advised that he would need to consider that possibility.

As Bill Emery and I returned to Abbotsford, we could only speculate as to the implications of what we had just heard. Apparently a mystery man would somehow form a part of the Driver defence, but with his own semen on Tanya's body, his bite-mark on her breast, and his admissions on the phone, how could that be possible? We shared what we had learned with prosecutors Neil Mackenzie and Sean Madigan, and they too could only wonder as to the meaning. Not surprisingly, no personal interview with Driver was ever granted to provide further details on this second suspect story. We would have to wait for court to hear this one.

As the court date approached, further indications of the defence's direction started to emerge. The defence elected trial by Supreme Court judge alone. In cases of murder, the accused has the choice of having their case heard and decided by a judge and jury or a judge alone. Depending on the nature of the case, an accused sometimes has a better chance of success with a sympathetic jury. Raping and murdering young girls is not the kind of sympathy-inducing case. Driver's choice of judge alone was not surprising; however, as the trial progressed, it would become even more obvious that a jury could never have been a choice to hear the story he intended to tell.

THE TRIAL PROCEEDS

Compared to other murder cases, this would not be an exceptionally long trial. Starting September 4, 1997, and concluding on October 16, 1997, it would take only twenty days in the courtroom. The presiding judge was Supreme Court Justice Wallace Oppal. Well respected as a fair-minded individual who took the time to carefully articulate his decisions, Justice Oppal had recently been the head of a commission inquiry into policing in British Columbia. He was no stranger to police operations and investigative procedures.

The trial took place in the Supreme Court Building in New Westminster, British Columbia. Typical of Canadian courts, the building in New Westminster is a three-story granite and marble structure with tall ceilings; long, heavily carpeted hallways; and rich wood, as well as featured walls displaying the pictures of past Supreme Court Justices. The hallways outside the courtrooms served as both passageways and waiting areas for witnesses and court visitors.

Not unlike other murder cases played out at this venue in the past, the victim families of Tanya Smith and Misty Cockerill, along with the family of the accused, Terry Driver, all shared the common hallways and waiting areas as the trial began. As investigators and witnesses, Bill Emery, Kevin Macleod, and I visited with the victim families as they arrived.

On the victim side, mothers, fathers, grandparents, aunts, and uncles were all present. On the accused side, Driver's mother, brother, and sisters were all in attendance. Driver's father and stepmother would arrive to witness the proceeding later. Driver's wife would only attend for a brief portion of the trial and then became understandably absent.

As with all criminal trials, witnesses are restricted from being in the courtroom until they have testified. This meant that Misty, other witnesses, and I myself would spend many hours awaiting our turns in the hallway.

On September 4, 1997, the trial commenced with preliminary applications. Much to our surprise, the defence agreed to allow the prosecution to enter a large amount of evidence by consent. Allowing evidence to enter by consent means that the Crown does not need to go through the process of calling all of the witnesses to establish a piece of evidence as fact.

In an agreed statement of facts, the defence admitted that:

- The semen on Tanya Smith was from Terry Driver
- Terry Driver was responsible for the bite-mark on the right nipple
- Terry Driver was responsible for all of the phone calls to the police
- Terry Driver stole and defaced Tanya Smith's headstone and placed it on the Radio Max car
- Terry Driver threw the letter attached to the wrench through the living room window of the house on Princess Street

- That it was Driver's fingerprint found on the tape used to wrap the letter to the wrench

Beyond this extensive list of admissions, Driver's lawyer made a plea to the judge that the contents of the letter attached to the wrench thrown through the window were not sufficiently relevant to the case and were too prejudicial to his client's case to be allowed as evidence. He submitted that the letter should not be allowed as evidence in this case.

For the prosecution, the letter was a valuable component the case against Driver. In addition to being his longest communication, it served to reconfirm and tie a number of issues together.

1. It alluded to dumping Tanya's clothing at the river, and that would lead to the natural assumption that he also dumped her body there
2. It confirmed the rotary stadium phone call
3. And most significantly, it admitted that the same baseball bat used on Misty and Tanya had been used in a previous attack—that previous attack additionally significant because it had taken place only ninety days prior to the attack on Tanya and Misty, and the site of the attack was at the front of the MSA Hospital and only two blocks away from the location where Tanya and Misty were attacked at the rear of the MSA Hospital.

The contents of the letter were very telling:

hello, it's me!!!

yes sir re, tanya's right nipple sure did taste good.

by the way tanya was wearing sandals that night and i threw them with her other stuff

she wasn't a bad lay either.

it was me that phoned from the rotary that night.

you cops getting a little pissed off yet.

hard to catch someone who is smart, not like some stupid crooks

that are no minds.

here are a few more of my conquests. i told you it wasn't my first.

it won't be my last either: i don't stay with the same MO. i have done more after these

ones also. go figure out which ones look in b.c., alta, and a few in Washington state.

how come you guys haven't clued into some of the incidents here in town the last

couple of years.

RE: bourquin cr. by mcDonalds, teen who was attempted sex assault i grabbed

her breasts and was about to gag her when she took off on me.

oriole dr. i almost had that woman beat senseless and was about to rape

her when a car came along. i sure don't need to be seen.

how about right across from the hospital. hey,, that was the same bat that was used on misty and tanya.

as soon as i saw it was an Indian i said no way, could have aids.

so i took her backpack found $200 in it and threw it
atop the old brick stored
**HEY GUYS I'M BAD
I WILL STRIKE AGAIN ONE DAY
I WILL NOT BE CAUGHT
I WILL NOT MOVE FROM ABBOTSFORD**
            **Bye guys this is the last time you here
from me till next time.
            GOOD LUCK!!**

To decide if the letter should be entered as evidence or not, Justice Oppal entered into a trial process known as a *voir dire*. The voir dire process, often referred to as "a trial within the trial," is used to determine the admissibility of a certain piece or pieces of evidence. In the voir dire, the judge will examine evidence related to the facts in question to determine if it was obtained legally and if it is sufficiently relevant to the case before the court to be considered as part of the evidence against the accused.

On the face of it, and from a commonsense perspective, it would seem that the letter, which was just another communication from Driver to the police, would be completely relevant to the case. Crown took the position that the letter represented evidence directly relevant to the attack on Misty and Tanya and that the attack on Misty and Tanya was specifically mentioned in reference to the baseball bat.

In regards to the three other attacks described in the letter, the crown called all three victims and police investigators, as witnesses. Each of the three cases was basically presented as a mini-trial to prove that each of the claimed offences had taken place as described in his letter. If accepted by the court, the contents of the letter could help to prove Driver's violent, sexually motivated propensity to attack women. As such proof, it would be "similar fact" evidence to the case before the court. Similar fact evidence is often accepted by Canadian courts where the accused is known to be responsible for a series of offences with similar fact patterns to the case before the court. On the basis of similar fact evidence, a judge can conclude that the accused has also committed the offence before the court. Crown submitted that the evidence should be accepted as proof of the truthfulness of the claims being made in the letter. This voir dire process took up the first days of the trial, and other witnesses sat impatiently waiting in the hallway.

For the defence, Mr. Orris argued that the content of the letter was insufficiently relevant to the case before the court and was therefore too prejudicial to be considered as part of the evidence for this trial.

Justice Oppal ruled that the majority of the letter making reference to other attacks on women was, as Mr. Orris argued, too prejudicial to be allowed as evidence; however, one portion of

hey,, that was the same bat that was used on misty and tanya.

The remainder of the letter, not referencing other attacks on women, would be admissible. To us, this ruling was most disappointing for the Crown case. We met with Sean Madigan and Neil MacKenzie to discuss the reasoning and the potential damage to the outcome of the case. As we discussed the issues, Mr. Madigan speculated that Justice Oppal could just be exercising caution in not presenting opportunities for appeal down the road. In a case like this, where there is so much other significant evidence, allowing the defence to be successful in an argument to disallow prejudicial evidence can be the safer, less-appealable course of action, for the judge to take. Even without the content of the letter, the case against Driver could still be proven on the evidence that the defence was allowing to enter by consent.

THE CASE FOR THE PROSECUTION

The next day of trial would be the first day outside of the voir dire. It would be the beginning of the entry of the Crown's evidence. Notwithstanding the agreement to allow evidence by consent, the Crown would still go through a process of calling witnesses to enter all the pieces of evidence. Like the careful construction of a puzzle, the pieces were fitted into their place for the judge to see and hear the fact pattern.

One of the first pieces would be Misty setting the stage for the events that would follow. Although the defence had consented to the entry of a substantial amount of evidence, that evidence did not include the critical testimony of Misty Cockerill. Now, nearly two years after the attack, Misty was an attractive, confident eighteen-year-old. Physically, she had almost fully recovered from her injuries, but it would still be an emotional nightmare to take the stand and face her attacker. As we visited in the courthouse hallway in the days leading up to her taking the stand, she demonstrated the same strength of character that had made her pick up the bat and hit her attacker instead of running away, the same spirit of survival that helped her find her way to the emergency ward and stay conscious long enough to report that her friend was still in trouble. She was a survivor and a fighter who had carried herself to this point. She would be a solid witness. Driver truly picked the wrong victim in this girl. I would like to have been in the courtroom the day that Misty took the stand; unfortunately, because I was waiting to testify, I was excluded.

From reports heard later, her testimony was clear and confident. She provided the story of her and Tanya's encounter with the attacker who stepped out from the bushes. She recounted the act of sexual assault on Tanya and her own attempt to fight back against the attacker, resulting in the vicious beating. She told the court about awaking semi-conscious and getting up from the ground, feeling her way along a chain-link fence, and finally stumbling through the front doors of the emergency ward.

She was questioned: Had anyone helped her get to the emergency ward? Her answer was certain: No, she got there alone.

When asked if her attacker was in the courtroom, she looked him straight in the eye and pointed to Terry Driver. Misty later told me that she kept her eyes fixed on Driver throughout most of her testimony. Much to her surprise and disgust, his body-language responses to her answers were strange and inappropriate. As she told her story, he nodded and smirked and almost seemed to be getting some entertainment out of her testimony. She wondered to herself, as she testified, if he was so arrogant that he thought the judge could not see these antics.

In cross-examination, Misty faced questions of why she had not identified Driver in the photo lineup and why the composite drawings looked so different from Driver if he was the attacker. In spite of these questions, she remained solid in her testimony that she now recognized Terry Driver as her attacker from that night. Later, as she told me about her time on the stand, she explained that there was just something about his eyes that she could not mistake and would never forget.

After Misty set the stage, the parade of prosecution witnesses continued.

First, the fishermen who found Tanya's body in the Vedder River took the stand.

This was followed by the collection of the autopsy evidence by forensic pathologist Dr. Sheila Carlisle who added graphic detail to the chain of events. Tanya Smith had suffered extreme blunt-instrument trauma to the skull, resulting in life-threatening injuries. Semen samples were found on the vulva, saliva samples on the bite-mark to the right nipple, and fibers found on the eyebrow all set the stage for linking the crime back to Terry Driver and his vehicle.

Finally, and most significantly, Dr. Carlisle testified that the cause of death was drowning; evident from water found in the lungs. Despite the extreme injuries to the skull, Tanya was still alive when her body was placed facedown in the Vedder River.

The significant bite-mark to Smith's right nipple was examined by Dr. David Sweet and matched to Driver's teeth as the probable biter. This bite-mark match was verified and supported by the saliva DNA on the bite-mark that was matched to the DNA from semen on the vulva.

The DNA comparisons were much more certain than the probable bite-mark. Comparing to a DNA sample taken from Terry Driver, the semen was a match to a probability of 1 in 1.7 trillion. These numbers could leave no doubt that Driver was the person who left the semen.

Finally, the fibers found on Tanya's eyebrow were determined by hair and fiber experts to match the fiber residues found in the trunk of Terry Driver's car. This supported the speculation that Tanya's body had been transported to the Vedder River in the trunk of his vehicle.

As Crown continued entering the evidence of the taunting phone calls and the theft of Tanya's headstone, Mr. Orris was true to his commitment. The evidence was entered without challenge and only the occasional question of clarification.

My own evidence for the purpose of this trial would be limited. The day of the autopsy, October 17, 1995, I made the decision with the primary investigators, Emery and MacLeod, that the bite-mark would be kept confidential as holdback evidence. This point would be significant. The bite to the right nipple was the same piece of evidence Driver would select to reveal to convince police that he was the killer. Driver first used this holdback in the phone call that I recorded the day after the autopsy on October 18, 1995.

By his own admission in court, we later learned that Driver had made his first phone call to the police and was spoken to by Kevin MacLeod earlier on October 18. In this phone call he claimed to be the person who had driven Misty to the hospital after she was attacked.

After the strange phone call to MacLeod, we discovered that the recording system to the tip lines was not working, and as an interim measure, we hooked up tape recorders patched directly onto the telephone handsets.

The fact that the entire conversation of Driver's first recorded phone call was not complete would result in some cross-examination.

When I received the phone call on October 18, the first words that I heard were, "I know where the murder happened." I was not able to record these first words. As I turned on the tape recorder and tried to interrupt the caller, I gestured for silence in the task force office. He was clearly intent to talk uninterrupted, and I allowed the call to continue.

He continued, "Beside a walkway that runs north and south on a grassy knoll behind trees."

I was able to interject and ask, "Okay, sir. Where are you getting this from?"

The caller responded, "I'm the killer. Her right nipple tasted pretty good."

With this the caller hung up, and with the tape recorder still running, almost in disbelief, I uttered the words, "Wow, s***. Let's get a trace on this."

Mr. Orris questioned my certainty as to the first words being, "I know where the murder happened."

I was very certain, and immediately after the call, I recorded what I had heard in my notebook. The event of this phone call had been so shocking and unexpected that it was as if the details were burned into my memory. It was one of those moments in time that you could not forget even if you wanted to.

No need for melodrama; the court accepted my evidence as stated, and I was excused.

The case for the prosecution was soon completed. Evidence was before the court by consent and unchallenged that:

- Terry Driver's semen, saliva, and bite-mark were on Tanya Smith's body.
- Material from Driver's vehicle trunk had been found on Tanya's eyebrow.
- Driver had made phone calls to the police claiming to be the killer and threatening to kill again.
- Driver had stolen and defaced the headstone from Tanya's grave.
- And finally he had thrown a letter through the window of an Abbotsford home, and in that letter was the statement: "hey,, that was the same bat that was used on misty and tanya."

It was hard to imagine what possible defence could be made to the charges with such a body of evidence before the court.

THE CASE FOR THE DEFENCE

On the first day of the defence presentation, Mr. Orris commenced by delivering an extended monologue to prepare the court for what it was about to hear. He intended to call three doctors as witnesses. Two doctors were psychiatrists, and the third was a surgeon who was an expert on Tourette's syndrome. The doctors would provide the court with information about Driver's thinking processes and how these processes were affected by his afflictions with Tourette's syndrome, Attention Deficit Hyperactivity Disorder (ADHD), and Obsessive Compulsive Disorder. Mr. Orris made it very clear that these witnesses would not be the basis for a defence of insanity, but rather a means of creating an understanding of Terry Driver's unique way of thinking and interacting socially.

Along with the doctors, Driver's own mother would take the stand and outline the problems of his troubled childhood.

Orris went on to explain that as his first witness, he would call Terry Driver himself. He said Driver would tell the story of being out "scanner chasing," an expression that Driver used to describe the activity of driving around while listening to his police scanner and then finding the police calls.

On the night of the attack, Driver, out "scanner chasing," had called police around midnight and reported a man on a stolen bicycle. He met with a police officer to point out a location and complete the report. After leaving the police officer, he drove down to Bevan Avenue, and as he approached the rear of the Extended Care ward, he saw a man dressed in dark clothing exit the hedges and run across the road. Believing the man may have been involved in breaking and entering or breaking into cars, Driver pulled over and went through the hedges to view the area the man had come from. Upon sticking his head through the hedges, he could see the two girls, Cockerill and Smith, lying unconscious on the grassy area at the corner of the hedgerow. Cockerill was dressed and lying curled up; however, Smith was nude and lying with her legs spread. His first idea was to make a phone call for help, but he considered the implications of using his cell phone and becoming involved, so he decided that he should drive to the 7-Eleven one block to the east and use the pay phone. Driving away, he realized that he had not heard anything on his scanner that would indicate that the attack on the girls had been reported. The thought then occurred to him that he should return to the area and have sex with the unconscious girl.

He returned to the back area of the parking lot and had intercourse with the unconscious body of Tanya Smith. After a short time he ejaculated, and although he tried to pull out, he knew that some of his semen was left on her body. During the time that he was having intercourse with Smith, he could hear her breathing. Once he finished intercourse, he proceeded to suck on her breasts and her nipples. As he was sucking on her nipples, Smith had a convulsion, and in shock, Driver testified that he bit into her right nipple. At the time of this convulsion, Driver believed that Smith had stopped breathing and realized that his semen would be found on a dead girl.

He loaded Smith and all of her clothing and the baseball bat into the trunk of his car. He loaded Misty, still unconscious, into the front passenger's seat and drove her to the front of the MSA hospital, where he left her to be found. Continuing on, he took Tanya to the Vedder River, where he placed her body into the water, reasoning that doing so would wash away the evidence. After placing the body in the river, he unloaded his car, throwing the clothing into the bushes. He retained the baseball bat, which he later discarded as he drove down Number Three Road leaving the scene.

He then told the court that he went home and listened to his scanner and the radio, and the next morning, after his wife had gone to work, he took his two children back out to the Vedder River to see if the body had been found. Upon arrival, he found the police processing a crime scene.

Mr. Orris told the court that Driver made his first phone call to the police because he had heard a news release asking for information from anyone who might have helped Misty get to the hospital. He wanted to provide that information about helping Misty; however, when asked to identify himself, he panicked and hung up.

His second phone call was made to the police because he heard a media release that they were having trouble locating the attack site. When asked where he was getting the information from, he was taken aback and responded, "I'm the killer. Her right nipple tasted pretty good." Orris said Driver responded that way because by that time he believed that his failing to get Tanya Smith to the hospital had resulted in her death.

Orris offered that Driver would testify regarding the other calls that he was being driven by his compulsive disorder and was feeding off the media. He would say that he was responsible for stealing and defiling Miss Smith's gravestone, although he would not be able to say specifically why he did so.

Finally, Driver would admit to composing the letter that was attached to the wrench and subsequently throwing it through the window of the unrelated Abbotsford home.

As Mr. Orris closed his oration, Justice Oppal asked for clarification on the defence to the charges.

Justice Oppal inquired, "I just want to understand it. The defence to the murder count is that he didn't do it, and the defence to the attempted murder is that again he didn't do it but involved himself in a sexual assault, is that it?"

Orris responded. "He is responsible for her death in one sense. He put her in the river and she drowned, so he is responsible in that context."

Justice Oppal probed further. "My concern is that if he has admitted responsibility for her death, what will I expect to hear as far as the defence to the first-degree murder?"

Orris said, "You will hear, my lord, that when he put her in the river, he believed that she was dead at that point."

Justice Oppal, "So he had no intent?"

Orris said, "Exactly."

With this understanding established, the morning session adjourned.

THE WEB OF DECEPTION

On the morning session of the thirteenth day of trial, Terry Driver took the stand as the most critical witness to his own defence. In criminal law, a person on trial is not required to take the stand to testify in their own defence. It is the obligation of the Crown to prove the charge beyond a reasonable doubt; however, in this case there was so much evidence, including telephone admissions of, "I'm the killer." If there was going to be a defence made, it would have to include Terry Driver's explanation of the events.

Similar to his demeanor throughout the trial to date, his face reflected little emotion or affect. His characteristic twitching, apparently an ongoing symptom of his Tourette's syndrome, displayed itself intermittently. As he approached the stand, he glanced toward his family in their usual seats near the front of the courtroom on the right-hand side. There was a nod and the flicker of a smile as he stepped up into the witness box.

The long journey through his evidence would be guided

following the sequence of events that Mr. Orris had already outlined for the court. Driver proceeded to provide information, answering questions first about his childhood and upbringing, then placement into institutional care at the age of five. He provided the outline of his troubled childhood and later youth that included institutional abuse, family violence, and finally isolation from his family. Into his teen years, he revealed his early introduction to using prostitutes and trading food from the fast-food outlet where he worked for sexual favors. By the time he was in his late teens and had moved back with his father, he was using prostitutes on a regular basis. By this time his daily sexual fantasies fed a habit of compulsive masturbation. His own recollection of his childhood afflictions of Attention Deficit Hyperactivity Disorder and Tourette's syndrome included a regime of medications to gain control. In spite of these afflictions, he was able to proceed with his education and managed to make his way through trade school, apprenticing as a printer.

Married to his current wife in 1990, he was the father of two children. His hobbies were fishing and scanner chasing, the latter being the practice of driving around, listening to a police-frequency scanner, and attending police calls. He identified for the court his own scanner that was in evidence and listed the various police frequencies it was programmed to receive. Included in the list were Abbotsford Police, Chilliwack RCMP, and the RCMP Freeway Patrol.

By the time Mr. Orris directed his attention to the night of October 13, 1995, Driver had achieved a level of apparent comfort on the stand and was speaking clearly with only the occasional evidence of his characteristic facial tick.

With Orris showing him police photographs of the Bevan Avenue area where the girls were first confronted, Driver explained to the court that after pointing out a possible bicycle theft to the police, he decided that he would continue to listen to his scanner and do a sweep of the area.

Driving east on Bevan Avenue, he told the court that he saw a person running fast at an angle across Bevan coming from the area of the hedges behind the Bevan Lodge. He was unable to describe the person other than to say he assumed it was a male by the stance and the way they ran.

Curious as to what the person was running away from, Driver stated that he stopped his car and looked through the cedar hedge. This is the point at which he found the two young girls lying unconscious in the corner of the parking lot. Tanya, lying closest to him, was nude on her back with her legs spread. Misty was lying near her feet in a fetal position.

He could see a baseball bat laying a couple of feet away from Tanya's body. He told the court what he had seen left him panicked and awestruck. He walked back toward his car to call for help on his cell phone. Before he could dial 911, he had second thoughts about becoming involved in this incident. Knowing how the police worked, he was certain that he would be held as a suspect, and he did not want anything to do with that. The situation was beyond what he liked to do in his scanner chasing.

Instead of using his cell phone, he decided to drive down to the 7-Eleven store two blocks to the east and use the pay phone to make the call. As he drove down toward the mall, the picture of what he had seen, particularly the naked girl lying on the ground, kept popping into his mind. It then occurred to him that he had not heard anything over his scanner to indicate that anyone knew anything about what had happened. At this point he decided that he could drive back and find the place, have sex with the nude girl, and then go and make that anonymous call to the police. Driver detailed the route that he took his vehicle back to the parking lot behind the Bevan Lodge. He described how he parked his car and used it for concealment between the back of the lodge and the hedge corner where the girls lay unconscious.

Orris asked, "Concealment in what way?"

Driver responded matter-of-factly, "I was going to have sex with the person that was on the ground."

Orris, apparently looking for a different answer, rephrased, "Concealment from what?"

Driver responded, "Well, there's a building right beside the parking lot with windows to it."

Describing how Tanya was breathing in raspy breaths, he detailed the process of pulling down his own jogging pants and underwear and placing himself between her legs to have sex. Prompted by his lawyer to be specific, he testified to the graphic details of intercourse. It was remarkable to hear and see that neither the tempo of his speech nor the expression on his face changed as he provided the evidence. There was no tremor in his voice, no discernable emotion, embarrassment, shame, or remorse in his expression. He recounted the events as if he were describing a walk in the park or a trip to the grocery store. The nature of this man appeared to be transparent here; he was cold and calculating.

Driver would continue recounting the events as previously detailed by his lawyer.

As he finished having intercourse, he failed to stop in time, and he was aware the he had left semen in and on Smith's body.

He proceeded with his evidence. "As I was sucking on her breasts, she did something that I wasn't expecting to happen. The only way I can describe it is she went into a seizure or a convulsion and at that exact moment that she took a deep breath and started having a seizure, it scared me, and I bit into her breast. I backed away and started pulling up my pants. It lasted probably five, ten seconds, I would guess. She was just shaking on the ground, making gagging noises or something and just shaking. She then all of a sudden stopped. That breathing I was hearing before wasn't there anymore, that raspy sound. I assumed what I had just seen was that she died in front of me."

Orris: "All right. What did you do?"

Driver: "I'd now just gotten mixed up with something where a girl just died. I've just had sex with somebody who's just died. I didn't want to be at all connected with this now. As I was trying to figure out what I was going to do in a panicked state, I decided that because I realized that I had probably left semen inside of Tanya... that I was going to take her somewhere, put her in water that would wash anything off that would have been of me."

Driver went on to explain how he loaded Tanya's body, along with her clothing and the baseball bat, into the trunk of his car. Then he placed Misty into the front passenger's seat and drove her to the front of the MSA hospital where he placed her against a cement curb to supposedly be found and helped. Here it occurred to him that he should take

Tanya's body to the Vedder River where he had fished on many occasions.

The Vedder River, being a location some fifteen kilometers to the east of Abbotsford, Driver described the route taken to reach the freeway. Then, in a critical statement that Justice Oppal would later refer to as contradiction to his claims of panic, he testified, "I take a right at McCallum and start heading towards the highway on-ramp. At the same time I'm doing this, I've taken out my radar detector, set it up, and I've switched my scanner over to the Chilliwack Highway Patrol."

He continued to describe his trip and eventual arrival at the Vedder River, where he had fished on numerous occasion. Here he removed Tanya's body from the trunk of the car and placed it facedown into the waters of the river. Throwing her clothing into the bushes along the trail to the river, he got back into his vehicle and left the area with the baseball bat still in his front seat. As he proceeded away from the river area along Number Three Road, he started throwing items out the passenger window into the ditch. First he said he threw out the aluminum baseball bat. Then he threw other items of personal property from the trunk that he thought might be contaminated with the blood of the victim. The items included two towels, a pair of fishing gloves, and a baseball cap.

With this done, Driver told the court how he returned home after two a.m. and went to bed with his scanner on next to him, listening for any report of the attack on the girls. Not having slept much that night, he rose with his wife the next morning, and after she left for work, he inspected the trunk of his car. He found blood on the yellow carpet liner, the foam seal, and the bumper.

After removing the carpet and washing away other blood-stains on the car, he took his two young children with him and disposed of the carpet, throwing it in a ditch in an older area of Abbotsford. This done, he proceeded with his children back to the dyke of the Vedder River. He drove along the top of the dyke toward the area where he had dumped the body. As he approached the area, he could see an ambulance, police, and a silver coffin. He drove toward the crime scene until the road-way on the dyke was blocked by an ambulance. The ambulance attendant helped direct him as he turned his vehicle around on the narrow dyke road. Then, for some reason he could not explain, he used his cell phone to call his friend Cliff and let him know that the police were processing some kind of crime scene on the Vedder River near their fishing hole.

Mr. Orris moved Driver along in time to October 16 and 17. Orris reviewed press releases presented in evidence earlier by Constable Elly Sawchuk, the police media liaison officer.

Orris: "Now we have the press releases that we've reviewed through Miss Sawchuk, and she tells us that on the sixteenth and seventeenth of October, police were asking the public for assistance with respect to anyone who had seen these two young ladies between 8:00 p.m. Friday night and 8:00 a.m. on Saturday morning. Later on the seventeenth, she acknowledges that the police were asking for anybody who may have driven Miss Cockerill to the hospital or dropped her off to come forward. Did you hear any of that?"

Driver: "Yes, I did."

Orris: "Now, on October eighteenth, there were a number of calls made by yourself, is that correct?"

Driver : "Yes."

Orris: "And do you remember when it was that you made the first call, to the police I'm talking about now, telephone call?"

Driver: "Yeah, about eleven o'clock."

Orris: "Okay, and why was it that you made this call?"

Driver: "Because it was just reported on you know, in the news that they wanted to figure out how Misty had gotten to the hospital because no one knew for sure how she got there."

Driver elaborated on the content of this call answered by Corporal Kevin MacLeod.

Driver: "I remember some things, not too many. I told them that I was the one who had taken Misty to the hospital. He asked me who I was. I told him that I didn't want to get involved with this thing, and he came back to the effect, you know, well, you already are involved in this for taking her to the hospital. This is a serious thing that's happening. One girl's dead, the other one has been seriously hurt, so on, so forth like that. I got to the point where he started asking too many questions, got nervous, and just hung up."

Orris: "You were the person who had taken Misty to the hospital. Did you not expect that the police would ask you questions about that?"

Driver: "Actually, no, not really. It was just my intention to tell them, to fill that one piece of the puzzle that they didn't have."

Returning to work for the rest of the day, Driver told the

court about other calls he made after leaving work later in the afternoon.

Orris: "All right. Now, we have another call that takes place on October the eighteenth, and it takes place, as I understand it, according to the police evidence, at 1554 hours, I think it is. Yes, 3:54 in the afternoon. This is also a call that you made?"

Driver: "Yes."

Orris: "Okay. Now, this is a call that I refer to as the reference to 'the grassy knoll and the fence, driveway kind of thing' call. We can refer to it specifically, if you want, if that assists, but you made that call, correct?"

Driver: "Yes, I did."

Orris: "All right. Now, how did it come about that you made the call?"

Driver: "Well, I went to pick up my kids from daycare and started heading home. The news broadcasts were on, stating that the police still didn't know where the assault had happened, where the attack occurred, or anything like that, so on my way home, I stopped off at the pay phone across from MSA Arena and got out and made a phone call to fill in that other piece of puzzle that they needed."

Orris: "All right. Now, I want to deal with the question of time at this point. This call is made about 3:54 in the afternoon?"

Driver: "Yes."

Orris: "Okay. Had you by this time heard as to what Tanya's cause of death was?"

Driver: "I do not recall."

Orris: "Now, there was a press release to that effect on October the seventeenth and a comment on the eighteenth by Miss Sawchuk confirming that drowning was the cause of death in relation, I'm sorry, not a press release, but a comment by her on the eighteenth of October that drowning was the cause of death of Miss Smith that was released to the media sometime on October eighteenth. Do you have any recall as to whether or not you had heard that at that time?"

Driver: "Yes, I did."

Orris: "By the time you made the 15:54 call?"

Driver: "No, I do not."

Orris: "Okay. In any event, that call is on the same line, the tip line, do you recall that?"

Driver: "Yes."

Orris: "Okay. And your recollection is making that call to let them know where this had happened?"

Driver: "Yes, I did."

Orris: "And I believe you told us that it was from a pay phone across from the MSA Arena?"

Driver: "Yes, it was."

Orris: "Just to be clear, this is the second call you've made that day?"

Driver: "Yes."

Orris: "All right. You see in the transcript, 'Beside a walkway that runs north/south on a grassy knoll behind trees.' 'Okay, sir, where are you getting this from?' 'I'm the killer.' 'Her right nipple tasted pretty good,' and then, 'Wow, s***, let's get a trace on this,' from Inspector Gehl. Now, you've heard the tape, of course?"

Driver: "Yes."

Orris: "Recognize your voice?"

Driver: "Yes."

Orris: "Now, Inspector Gehl has not recorded the opening comments attributed to you. Do you recall what it was that you said in the opening comments at all?"

Driver: "I stated something to the fact that I knew where the assaults took place or where the two girls were assaulted or something like that. I did not say what he said I said."

Orris: "Okay. And what is it about what he said that you take exception to?"

Driver: "That I know where the murder happened."

Orris: "Okay. In any event, you continue on and you say, 'Beside a walkway that runs north/south on a grassy knoll behind trees.' Now you're describing the scene that you came upon, location of the scene that you came upon. Is that correct?"

Driver: "That's correct."

Orris: "Now, the question is, 'Okay, sir, where are you getting this from?' and then you say, 'I'm the killer. Her right nipple tasted pretty good.' Why did you say that?"

Driver: "Say what part?"

Orris: "'I'm the killer.'"

Driver: "At the time in my mind, I held myself responsible for her death because to me, she died at the scene through my neglect of not getting her to help instead of sexually assaulting her. To me, it was my fault she had died because of my neglect."

At this point Justice Oppal interrupted the questioning of the accused to ask for clarification on an obviously critical point.

Oppal: "So I want to get this right. You held yourself responsible for her death because you neglected to get her help and sexually assaulted her instead?"

Driver: "Yes."

Orris: "And as you've told us, you believe that she had died as a result of you not getting her help?"

Driver: "Yes."

Orris: "And doing to her what you've done, obviously, instead of getting her help?"

Driver: "That's correct."

Orris: "All right. You made the reference in this call to 'her right nipple tasted pretty good.' Why did you say that? Can you recall why you said that?"

Driver: "So the call wouldn't be held as a prank. I knew at the moment she had that seizure that I did bite into her and assumed that more than likely left a mark."

Orris: "So you simply said that because you wanted the police to know it wasn't a prank call?"

Driver: "That's right."

Orris: "Now, we have a lot of evidence from the various police officers that this was holdback information, that it wasn't published. You didn't hear it or any transmission of this kind of evidence of this kind of fact over the scanner?"

Driver: "No, I did not."

Orris: "It is something you knew because you were responsible for it?"

Driver: "That's correct."

Orris: "All right. Now, following that phone call, which is quite short, we have another phone call that occurs at about 6:09 p.m., but after you make the phone call from opposite the MSA Arena, what do you do then?"

Driver: "I headed home. I turned on the scanner as soon as I got home. I'd heard that they had called for Ident to come down to the telephone."

Orris: "Where did you hear that?"

Driver: "Over the scanner. To come down to the phone across from the MSA or something like that. I decided I'd go and take a look and see if they had gone to the spot where I told them where the assault had taken place."

Orris: "Yes."

Driver: "My wife wasn't home yet, so I put the kids in the car and went for a drive down to the MSA Arena area. I drove past the area where they were fingerprinting. I made a left onto Bevan and drove all the way down to where the assault had taken place to see if they were there yet, and they weren't there yet. I then proceeded to go home after that."

Orris: "Now, once you got home, about what time are we talking about?"

Driver: "Could be about 4:30."

Orris: "Okay. And what happens then?"

Driver: "Well, the time passes. It comes about five o'clock. I put the news on and I'm watching the news. That's when I actually recall actually seeing and hearing the news report coming over stating that she had died from drowning."

Orris: "And what is going through your mind when you hear that?"

Driver: "I was in shock. It was like someone had punched me in the stomach and ripped my guts out type of feeling. I couldn't believe what I was actually hearing. Waited until my wife came home. I can't remember when she came, but after a while, I decided I wanted to go for a drive because I was upset, so I got in my car and drove down to the Matsqui Trails beside the Fraser River."

Orris: "Okay. I just want to go back here. Tell me why you were upset?"

Driver: "Because it's now that I've realized to the fact now it was at my hands that she died. I've now realized it was through my putting her in the water that she drowned, and it was my fault that that happened."

Orris: "All right. So you told us that you were upset. You went for a ride or a drive. Did you take your scanner?"

Driver: "Yes."

Orris: "Did you have it on?"

Driver: "Yeah."

Orris: "And you went where?"

Driver: "Down to the Matsqui Trails, right beside the Fraser River."

Orris: "Okay. What happens when you get down there?"

Driver: "I went down there because I like being by the river. It's peaceful, it's calming, and it's soothing. It allows me to think about things and straighten things out and stuff like that. I went down there, sat for a while. I can't remember offhand what I was thinking or anything watching the fishermen there, seeing what they were doing, and then I started driving away. As you go off the Matsqui Trail and go onto the main road, there was a phone booth that was sitting there. I stopped the car, went to the phone booth, and made another phone call."

Orris: "Now, could you think of anything at this point that you may have heard on the scanner or anything that was in your mind that prompted you to do that?"

Driver: "Nothing over the scanner."

Orris: "Anything in your mind that prompted you to make that call at that time other than seeing the phone booth?"

Driver: "No. I can't recall anything."

Orris: "All right."

Driver: "I just remember that that's the first time I started dialing 911."

Orris: "Okay. Now, when you dialed 911 on this occasion, did you have anything in your mind as to what you were going to say?"

Driver: "No, it just came to me what to say after I asked for police. At the time, no, there was nothing in my mind what I was going to say. When it was transferred over to the police, that's when it came into my head about if I'd be stupid enough to leave fingerprints behind."

Orris: "Of course, you'd driven by the scene of the previous phone call earlier."

Driver: "Yes."

Orris: "Okay. This call, like the others, is quick, and then I take it after saying what you said, you hung up?"

Driver: "Yes, I did."

The end of the court day was near, and Driver went on to detail his third recorded phone call to 911 that day, this final call being the one where he claimed to be the killer and threatened that he would be driving around looking for someone else.

He continued to tell the court that the ideas and verbal content for his calls just came to him as he was making the calls. When asked why, in this final call, he claimed to be the killer, he told the court that by that time he had realized that Tanya had died at his hands. He was actually the person who had killed her by putting her in the river. His threat to kill again in this call was intended to make the police work harder on the case.

The next morning, Driver's examination in chief continued with his explanation to the court of how he had attended Tanya Smith's funeral.

Orris: "All right, and tell us why you attended the funeral on October twenty-first."

Driver: "It was just my way of thinking of dealing with what happened and to say, in my way, sorry to her."

From here Mr. Orris moved on to the Halloween-night phone call from Gigi's Sports Bar. In explaining how this call came about, Driver offered that he had taken his children out trick-or-treating and then went out scanner chasing.

Driver: "I was just, you know, driving around. I ended up down in the lower part of Abbotsford by the Highway Eleven on-ramp area. As I was driving down Sumas Way, just passing by Gigi's Sports Bar, I saw the phones there and just pulled in. I pulled up beside the telephones and just parked. Went up to the pay phone, dialed 911, operator came on, and I just said the first thing that came into my mind. I don't recall why I said what I said, but I do distinctly remember the feeling of being angry with the Abbotsford Police. But I don't know why."

Orris: "All right. What you say in this phone call is—the phone is answered,

Operator: '911 Emergency, do you need police, fire, ambulance?'
Caller: 'Police.'
Operator: 'What's your emergency?'

Caller:	'Tonight I'm not going to bite her right nipple, I'm going to bite her right…, eat her f****** c***.'
Operator:	'When's this going to happen?'
Caller:	'Oh, it's happening…. (unintelligible).'
Operator:	'Oh, you guys.'

Orris: "End of transmission. That's the call that was made. Now, as far as what you said there, did you have any plans on what you were going to say at all?"

Driver: "No."

Orris: "You simply said what came into your mind?"

Driver: "Yes, I did."

Orris: "Now, you said you remember being angry at the police."

Driver: "Yes."

Orris: "This time. Are you able to now tell us why you were angry at the police?"

Driver: "No. No."

Orris moved Driver on directing his testimony through the events surrounding the release of the voice tapes to the media. He then went on to discuss the release of George Evenden and the media announcement confirming the elimination of Evenden as a suspect through DNA analysis. Driver confirmed that he was aware of the events and had been following this through the media.

Orris moved Driver along to explain the events surrounding the theft and defacing of the gravestone. On the morning of February 17, Driver explained that he had headed out to go fishing.

Driver: "I then headed down towards Old Abbotsford to

take the Number Eleven Highway area. I drove down to the Highway Eleven, started going down the road. I knew where the cemetery was she was buried in. As I was driving down Highway Eleven, I noticed a sign there pointing to it and just turned over onto the road and went to the cemetery."

Orris: "And again, was this something that you, before seeing the sign, had planned to do?"

Driver: "No, it wasn't. I was actually fully dressed in my fishing equipment at the time."

Orris: "Okay. And when you saw this sign directing you to the cemetery, what was your plan at that point?"

Driver: "I can't recall what it was at the time."

Orris: "All right. So you went to the cemetery. You went to her grave obviously."

Driver: "Yes."

Orris: "Okay, and tell us what happened."

Driver: "I got out of the car, walked over to the gravesite. I can't recall really what I thinking at the time. The only thing I can honestly say I know I was thinking was that I wanted to put the gravestone at the spot where she had actually died."

Orris: "That was by the river?"

Driver: "That was by the river."

Orris: "So what did you do?"

Driver: "I went back to the car, got a crowbar out of the car, and tried moving the headstone. Eventually it came loose. I picked it up and walked it over to the car.

I put it in the backseat of my car."

Orris: "Okay. So the headstone is in the backseat of your car?"

Driver: "Yes."

Orris: "Is it facing up, down, how is it facing?"

Driver: "It's facing up."

Orris: "And are you still dressed in your fishing gear?"

Driver: "Yes, I am."

Orris: "So where do you go from there?"

Driver: "I started driving back up Highway Eleven towards Abbotsford, towards Highway One, you know, figuring I'm going take it to the river. As I'm driving up, getting close to Highway One, I'm thinking, you know, it's getting too late in the morning with the weight of the headstone. There'd be no way I could actually walk it all the way to the river's edge without someone seeing me doing it."

Orris: "Okay. So what happens?"

Driver: "I start thinking, *Well, what else am I going to do with it?* I then decided that I'd take it and put it over the memorial site that was laid up at the park on Bevan Street. I got to that area. The only parking spot that was there was around by the school, which means I would have to walk about seventy-five feet over towards the tree where the memorial was."

Mr. Orris clarified that the memorial Driver was speaking of was actually several blocks from the attack site in a park near Godson School.

Driver continued: "Yes. As I'm driving up South Fraser Way, I'm still thinking, *You know, what am I going to do with the headstone?* I noticed a sign for 85 Radio Max, and it pops into my head, *Well, this is the best place as any to put it now.* I drive up into the back parking lot. I see an 85 Radio Max car there, and I park beside it."

Orris clarified that all of this happened around two

o'clock in the afternoon, just prior to the call being made to the Radio Max disc jockey.

Driver: "But I didn't want it to be just left there and someone think, you know, it was just done as a prank or something, so I was going to start writing stuff on the headstone."

Orris: "All right. And you did this?"

Driver: "Yes, I did."

Orris: "And the writing we see on the headstone, that was all done—the handwriting, I'm talking about, of course, was all done at that time?"

Driver: "Yes."

Orris: "And so how does it come about that you write on it?"

Driver: "Well, my car has bucket seats, so I moved over to the passenger's-side seat. I pulled down the armrest. I pull down the driver's-side chair and just reach over into the backseat and start writing on it."

Orris: "All right, and what were you using?"

Driver: "A pen."

Orris: "Okay. And the writings are obviously around the Smiths' photograph, or at least her etching on the white areas around it, on her face, correct?"

Driver: "Yes."

Orris: "And why again did you do those writings?"

Driver: "To show that, you know, it wasn't just a prank. At that time too the media had started throwing a lot of their sensationalism into what's happening here, and I was feeding off of that too."

Orris: "I'm not quite sure what you mean by that, 'Feeding off of it.'"

Driver: "The attention, I guess, that it was generating."

Orris: "And all the writing[s] on there are yours?"

Driver: "Yes."

Orris: "And there's a reference, of course, there's an arrow pointing to her breast, correct?"

Driver: "That's correct."

Orris: "And why did you do that particular writing?"

Driver: "That would specifically say that it was from me—"

Justice Oppal interjected: "Are you saying—excuse me for interrupting, are you saying that you did this because you started to feed off the media-generated attention?"

Driver: "Yes."

Justice Oppal: "You got caught up in all of this?"

Driver: "Yes, I did."

Orris: "Now, once you've completed the writing, what occurs then?"

Driver: "I get out of the car. I take the headstone out of the car."

Orris: "Tell us what you do."

Driver: "I reach in. I pull it out, resting—I believe it was resting against my knees or something. I back out in a squat position and lift it up and just move it over to the car, the same way I'd carried it originally."

Orris: "When you say the car, you mean the Radio Max car?"

Driver: "Yes."

Orris: "Okay. And what did you do then?"

Driver: "I put it on top of the hood, and I don't remember it now, but I guess what I'd done is push it up higher up onto the car."

Orris: "All right. So you put it there. What do you do now?"

Driver: "I just look around the parking lot as I'm walking towards my car and just get into the car and drive away."

Orris: "All right. What do you do then?"

Driver: "I drive down South Fraser Way. It wasn't my intention on making a phone call, just leave it there, but as I got to the corner of Trethewey and South Fraser Way, there's a pay phone that sits right there at the corner. I just pull in, dialed 85 Radio Max number, and told them to go look out in the parking lot on their car."

Orris: "All right. You're driving away from the parking lot."

Driver: "Yes."

Orris: "And you don't have any thought about making a phone call?"

Driver: "No, I did not."

Orris: "Well, when did that thought come into your mind?"

Driver: "As soon as I saw the phone booth."

Orris: "So what did you do after that?"

Driver: "Got back in the car and went home."

Orris: "All right. Now, the next significant date, of course, is the next day or later that day, are you listening to the radio, watching television, dealing with the papers?"

Driver: "Yes."

Orris: "Do you see any of the coverage in response to your placing the gravestone on the Radio Max car?"

Driver: "Yes, I did."

Orris: "Okay. And then we have a call on February the 19 of 1996, a call to 911."

Driver: "It'd be a Monday."

Orris: "All right. Well, let's deal with that, okay. You're right, I think the nineteenth is a Monday, according to my calculations or at least my calendar."

Driver: "Yes."

Orris: "That would have been a working day for you normally, is that correct?"

Driver: "That's correct."

Orris: "Okay. We're dealing with the telephone call that occurs about 2112 hours."

Driver: "Yes."

Orris: "Twelve minutes after nine at night?"

Driver: "Okay."

Orris: "Does that accord with your recollection?"

Driver: "Yes."

Orris: "So then tell us how that occurs. Where are you prior to this—before this telephone call?"

Driver: "Bowling. I was just coming back from dropping off our babysitter at her house."

Orris: "All right."

Driver: "And drove past Rotary Stadium. I know pay phones that were in Rotary Stadium and just drove up to where the pay phone was at Rotary Stadium."

Orris: "All right. Now, again, this telephone call, was that something that you'd planned to do that evening?"

Driver: "No, it wasn't. It was just a thought that came into my head as I was passing by Rotary Stadium from dropping off the babysitter that I remembered pay phones being there."

Orris: "So what did you do then?"

Driver: "I pulled into the parking lot close by where the concession stands are and the phone booth, walk over to the phone booth, dial 911, say whatever it is there that I said, and walked back to the car and drove away and went home."

Orris: "Now, again, this is a very short conversation. The complaint taker answers, '911 emergency, do you need police, fire or ambulance?' And then you say, 'How'd you like the present I gave you guys, huh?' Complaint taker, 'I'm sorry, sir, I can't hear you, sir.' You say, 'How'd you like the present I gave you guys?' Complaint taker, 'I'm sorry, I can't. ...' You say, 'It won't be the last.' Complaint taker, 'Okay, sir, just a minute.' That's the end of the call. Again, when you made that call, did you have any thought in your mind to what you were going to say?"

Driver: "No."

Orris: "But obviously you were—you directed your comment in reference to the present was the gravestone?"

Driver: "Yes. As I was driving to and even walking up to the pay phone, I don't remember what I was thinking at the time, but as I picked up the phone and dialed 911, that's when it came to me to say something about the headstone itself."

Orris: "Okay. You hang up the phone. Where do you go from there?"

Driver: "Home."

Orris: "Do you hang around to see if the police attend or anything of that sort?"

Driver: "No, I didn't. I just drove out past Rotary Stadium off of Trethewey, which you have to go past anyways, and just went home."

Orris moved Driver to discuss the incident of throwing the wrench with the letter attached through the window of the Princess Street home.

Orris: "Now, I want to next deal with the twenty-first of February. We're now talking, I think a Wednesday, and we're talking about this note and a pair of wrench and this envelope that goes through the window of this house. That's what I want to talk about. Okay?"

Driver: "Okay."

Orris: "Now, tell us how that comes about. We're dealing with the twenty-first of February. Tell us about that."

Driver: "As I was saying before, I was starting to feed off what the media was saying, to the fact that, you know—and to the police that the person isn't in Abbotsford anymore, that they're making this person out to possibly be a deranged psychopath, a real bad-guy type of person and just—a thought occurred to me to make up a note—a letter and give the media exactly what they wanted. When I was making the note, I was intending the note to actually be given to the media itself."

Orris: "All right. And, of course, everything else—I shouldn't say everything else, but one of the obvious responses to you, I guess, to what you did with the gravestone and the phone calls was that the media get them?"

Driver: "Yes."

Orris: "Okay. Now, the note itself, describe to me how you came to prepare that?"

Driver: "It was just a thought that occurred to me. I just sat down in front of the computer and started typing."

Orris: "This is the computer in you home?"

Driver: "Yes."

Orris: "How long did it take you?"

Driver: "I don't recall."

Orris: "We're dealing not only with the note, but did you think, for instance, that you wanted this note to—when it was given to the media or at least received by the police to want them to know it was coming from you?"

Driver: "Yes, it was. Yes, I did."

Orris: "There's a reference to, 'Tanya's right nipple, sure did taste good.'"

Driver: "Yes."

Orris: "That was, in effect, telling the police who this note was from?"

Driver: "That's correct."

Orris: "Now, once you typed up this note, what did you do with it?"

Driver: "Put it in an envelope. Put a wrench to it and taped it up."

Orris: "Okay. And what did you do with the note?"

Driver: "I put it in the envelope."

Orris: "And did you collect anything else to put in the envelope?"

Driver: "Yes, I did. I got some newspaper articles."

Orris: "And where were those from?"

Driver: "Newspapers."

Orris: "And how come you had those?"

Driver: "There were just—one was just the local paper that was sitting around the house, and another one was back in the eighties that I had forgotten about that I even had."

Orris: "So you extracted some parts, I guess, from the '85 paper?"

Driver: "Yes."

Orris: "We have pictures of Misty and Miss Smith that are also included in the note?"

Driver: "Yes."

Orris: "All right. Where did those come from?"

Driver: "Probably from the local newspapers."

Orris: "Now, I can show it to you, but on the photograph of Miss Cockerill, there's some writing (referencing "One day Misty" printed across the forehead of the photograph)?"

Driver: "Yes."

Orris: "Is that your writing?"

Driver: "Yes, it is."

Orris: "Do you remember putting that on?"

Driver: "No, I do not."

Orris: "So you have no recollection?"

Driver: "I have no recollection of writing that on there."

Orris: "All right. But it's your handwriting?"

Driver: "Yes, it is."

Orris: "Now, once you put these items into the envelope, what do you do with the envelope?"

Driver: "I write on it, thinking, you know, by putting what I put on it that would get immediate police attention."

Orris: "Now, we have Exhibit Fifty-eight, which is the envelope, the blue envelope. On one side of it is written 'Abby.' I guess it's intended to be Abby, A-b-b-y, is that correct?"

Driver: "Yes."

Orris: "And 'Killer. Call 911,' and then below that, 'From the.' That's all your writing, I take it?"

Driver: "Yes."

Orris: "Okay. Now, there's a drawing of some kind on the left which, can you tell me what that is?"

Driver: "I don't know."

Orris: "You don't have any recollection of what that is?"

Driver: "No, I do not."

Orris: "On the back is written 'From the killer. Call 911.'"

Driver: "Yes."

Orris: "That's your writing?"

Driver: "Mm hmm."

Orris: "Okay. And then you taped the pliers to it?"

Driver: "Yes."

Orris: "And you taped it to this note?"

Driver: "Yes."

Orris: "Well, what was your plan as you were doing this? Tell me."

Driver: "To throw it through the window of the Community Police building down on Essendene Avenue."

Orris: "That's not the police station?"

Driver: "No."

Orris: "So what did you do then?"

Driver: "I get in my car and drive away from there."

Orris: "From your home."

Driver: "From my home, yeah."

Orris: "You've got the note with you?"

Driver: "Yes."

Orris: "Where do you go?"

Driver: "I drive down to the Community Police Station. I can't recall why I changed my mind from there. I think I remember there was just too many people around at that time, too much traffic and stuff."

Orris: "Okay."

Driver: "I then started driving around and trying to decide what I was going to do, you know, where I was going to take it. At one point actually I even thought of going to the actual police station, but I passed that out of my mind as soon as that thought came into my mind. I eventually ended up in a residential area and decided this was as good a place as any to do it."

Orris: "Can you remember when you picked that house? Was there anything significant about the house at all?"

Driver: "No."

Orris: "So tell us what you do when you decide to dispose of the device, obviously throwing it through the window of this house?"

Driver: "I stopped the car. I get out. I walk up to the window and throw it through the window and come back to my car and drive away."

Orris: "And what time of day is this we are talking about?"

Driver: "Ten o'clock, I guess. I don't really recall the exact time."

Orris: "Now, again, I take it that you want to see what reaction this causes as far as the media is concerned?"

Driver: "Yes."

Orris: "You're expecting the media to get this note?"

Driver: "Yes."

Orris: "Do you follow what happens thereafter, as far as watching the media or reading the media or listening to the media?"

Driver: "Yes."

Orris: "Terry, I wanted to ask you a few more questions about this note. When you say that you typed it up on your computer, I take it that you also printed it out on your printer, is that correct?"

Driver: "Yes."

Orris: "Now, I want to deal with its contents, if I can. We have the first part of it, 'Hello, it's me,' exclamation marks, 'Yessiree, Tanya's right nipple sure did taste good.' Why are you writing that?"

Driver: "Tell them it's from me."

Orris: "Okay. And then you have a brackets, 'by the way, Tanya was wearing sandals that night and I threw them with her other stuff,' closed brackets. Now, why did you type that?"

Driver: "Because I remember hearing something about they were concerned they didn't know what kind of shoes she was wearing that night and nothing had been put on the media that anything was found."

Orris: "All right. And you say, 'She wasn't a bad lay either.' Now, why did you write that?"

Driver: "I guess egging-the-police-on type thing."

Orris: "'It was me that phoned from rotary that night. You cops getting a little pissed off yet? Hard to catch someone who is smart, not like some stupid crooks that are no-minds.' Why did you write all that?"

Driver: "Just as a way to get the police to pick up their pace, to investigate it basically. More as like to egg them on to get them going."

Orris: "All right. At the bottom of the note you have in capitalized, 'Hey guys, I'm bad.' Do you have any thought as to why you would type that?"

Driver: "No. Just something there to make it stand out."

Orris: "Okay. 'I will strike again one day.' This is all capitalized. Can you help us as to what was in your mind when you typed that?"

Driver: "Well, basically, that area there is more so for the press, I would say, because they've laid on through the last month or two that they've made this person out to be real bad, someone to fear."

Orris: "You state, 'I will not be caught. I will not move from Abbotsford.' Why did you type that?"

Driver: "Because they suspected that the person had moved away from Abbotsford."

Orris: "Then you write, 'Bye, guys. This is the last you hear from me 'til next time.' And then at the bottom you've written in capital letters, 'Good luck' with exclamation marks. What did you mean when you wrote, 'Good luck'? Good luck in relation to what?"

Driver: "Catching me basically."

Orris: "Now, following the throwing of the note through the window, I take it you're still dealing with or following this through the media?"

Driver: "Yes."

Orris: "Okay. Do we have any further phone calls between February twenty-first and when you were arrested?"

Driver: "No."

Orris: "Any particular reason why not, can you tell us?"

Driver: "No."

Orris: "Now, when the police first contacted you, do you recall that date?"

Driver: "It was Tuesday, I think, May third or before. No, it wasn't May third. No, I don't remember."

Orris: "All right. First part of May sometime."

Driver: "Yeah."

Orris: "Okay. How did they contact you?"

Driver: "Sergeant Emery and Corporal McLeod came to my door, knocking at the door."

Orris: "And did they identify themselves?"

Driver: "Yes, they did."

Orris: "Did they tell you why they were there?"

Driver: "Yes, they did."

Orris: "And did they ask you to cooperate with them or supply anything to them?"

Driver: "Yes, they did."

Orris: "You advised them that you wanted to talk to a lawyer?"

Driver: "Yes."

Orris: "And was that generally the conversation that you had with them at that time?"

Driver: "Basically. They were asking, you know, where I was on Halloween. They wanted to take a look at my car."

Orris: "Before you allowed them to do any of that, you told them you wanted to talk to a lawyer?"

Driver: "Yes."

Orris: "Now, you did so, did you not, after that?"

Driver: "Yes, I did."

Orris: "Okay. And eventually, some days later you attended at the police station with your lawyer at that time?"

Driver: "Yes, I did."

Orris: "A Mr. Harris?"

Driver: "Yes."

Orris: "What did you understand you were going to do when you went to the police station with Mr. Harris?"

Driver: "Supply fingerprints."

Orris: "All right. Mr. Harris supplied a letter, I think, to the police. Mr. Harris had advised you against that, correct?"

Driver: "That's correct."

Orris: "And notwithstanding that advice, you went to the police station and you supplied them with your fingerprints?"

Driver: "Yes."

Orris: "Okay. When you were there to do that, what did you think would happen?"

Driver: "That I was going to be arrested."

Orris: "Okay. And you were?"

Driver: "Yes."

Orris: "Had you made any arrangements in anticipation of that?"

Driver: "Yes, I did."

Orris: "What did you do?"

Driver: "I gave my wallet and jewelry and all my other personal stuff to my wife."

Orris: "And you then went to the police station and they took your fingerprints, and, as we've heard, you were arrested almost immediately after that?"

Driver: "That's correct."

Orris: "And you've been in custody since that time, is that correct?"

Driver: "That's correct."

With this, the offence-related portion of Driver's evidence ended, and Mr. Orris led him through providing samples of DNA and a bite impression after being taken into custody.

Orris then directed Driver's testimony to the recollection

of his childhood, his relationship with his parents, and his placement in institutional care. Leading him again through his late teens and early twenties, Driver revealed his experiences working for restaurants in the Granville Street area of Vancouver. As a restaurant employee, he took advantage of opportunities to trade food for drugs and sexual favors. This led to his continued use of prostitutes three to four times per month, even after he married and moved to Abbotsford.

Driver recounted his education and apprenticeship into the printing trade. He then testified about his 1989 diagnosis with Tourette's syndrome and some of the subsequent treatments.

He confirmed for the court that he had married his current wife in 1990, and their children were born in 1991 and 1992.

As Orris delved into Driver's relationship with his parents, Driver seemed to become evasive and offered that he "really didn't recall a lot."

Orris reminded Driver that he would be calling his mother to the stand to testify about his relationship with his father in particular.

Driver then conceded that he remembered being yelled at a lot and hit a few times by his father for "the bad habits that I used to do." These bad habits were not expounded on in Driver's testimony.

Orris then led Driver through testimony, pointing out that he did not have tattoos on his forearms; however, he did have tattoos on his shoulder, his leg, and one above his heart. He also told the court about the accidental amputation of the upper section of his left little finger in a 1986 elevator accident.

With these final pieces in place, it was now the prosecutor's turn to cross-examine Driver on his testimony.

For those of us who had been in the courtroom throughout Driver's testimony, the strategy was becoming clearer. Driver had woven his story around the known and provable points of evidence in this case. The story that he was not the person who had attacked Tanya and Misty presented an alternate possibility for the court to consider.

He was willing to admit to being the rapist of an unconscious girl to avoid the first-degree murder implications of being the attacker. According to him, he believed that Tanya had died during his sexual encounter. Her death was the result of injuries inflicted by someone else. He only learned that she had died as a result of drowning days later in a media release.

He initially felt responsible for her death because he had failed to get her medical attention, and then, when he learned she had died from drowning, he realized that he was responsible for her death. The argument would be no intent to kill.

Initially driven by the desire to provide the police with missing pieces of information, he started making phone calls, providing information about Misty getting to the hospital and the location of the attack site.

His later phone calls and communications were driven by anger at the police and a desire to make police work harder on the investigation. His admissions in phone calls claiming to be the killer were driven by his feelings of being responsible for Tanya's death.

Could the court believe his story?

In cases like this, where an accused testifies and provides an alternate explanation for the facts before the court, the court is obligated to give full consideration to the explanation provided.

Was Driver's version of the events plausible? Was Driver's testimony credible? Would there be a reasonable doubt? These were the questions that Justice Oppal would need to consider. If the story was judged to be believable, and if Driver was considered a credible witness, the verdict could be second-degree murder or even manslaughter. Challenging Driver's version of the events and attacking Driver's credibility was now the task for Prosecutor Sean Madigan.

Prior to beginning his cross-examination of Driver, Mr. Madigan made application to Justice Oppal to allow two additional points to be addressed in the cross-examination. The first would be the reference in the letter to the murder weapon, and the second would be to allow the cross-examination of Driver on character evidence.

Justice Oppal deliberated on the case the law presented and the arguments of the prosecution and defence.

Justice Oppal: "All right. Thank you. The Crown has applied to cross-examine the accused on his character. The evidentiary basis for making the application is contained in a portion of the accused's examination-in-chief, where he said, in reference to the acts of violence, words to the effect that 'he could not fathom himself doing something like this. The thought of the acts revolted him.' The Crown argued that in uttering those words, the accused has put his character in issue. To put it another way, it is argued that, in essence, the accused, by making those statements, has said that he is a person of good character. The law relating to character evidence is clear. The evidence of bad character of an accused is not admissible unless an accused chooses to put his or her character at issue. This is generally done by leading evidence of good character.

The law relating to character evidence is a law of longstanding. (Justice Oppal reviews points of the various cases.)

"In examining the evidence given by the accused in this case, there is no way that I could conclude that he put his good character in issue. While it is not always clear as to what constitutes character evidence, one thing is clear that there must be some clear and equivocal evidence pursuant to which a trier of fact could conclude that a person is putting his or her character in issue. There must be more than an oblique reference to character. I cannot conclude from the statements that were made here that this accused was intending to put his character in issue. I pause here to note that intention is not a prerequisite, of course, to putting one's character in issue, but I must look at his evidence as a whole and put that statement into proper context.

"I cannot conclude from his evidence that in any way he intends to convey to this Court that he is a person of good character. Accordingly, the Crown will not have leave to lead evidence of bad character."

Madigan: "What about the relevance now, my lord, of the murder weapon? Is it relevant or not?"

Justice Oppal: "What do you say to that, Mr. Orris? You didn't address that in your argument. The Crown says that because he (Driver) has made reference to the weapon and that weapon has been referred to (in the letter), that ought now to be admissible."

Orris: "I'm sorry. I'm just not sure what—there's a reference in the note, 'That was the same bat that was used on Misty and Tanya.' As far as that portion of the note was concerned, certainly I have no difficulty with it going in."

Justice Oppal: "All right."

Orris: "But that would be only part of that note, in my submission, that should go in as a result of his evidence."

Madigan: "It would be nonsensical to put the remainder of the end of a sentence and not the beginning. We have to be able to put things in that he had possession of during an incident across from the hospital. He says in this particular document that is the same bat which he had then, which he then also had on the night of the fourteenth."

Justice Oppal (to Mr. Orris): "Do you need a moment?"

Orris: "Well I'm just—my lord, I'll just be quite frank. I'm just trying to think—I may need a moment—whether the first part of the sentence makes any difference or not. If I may have a moment."

Justice Oppal: "All right. Think about it."

Adjournment

Orris: "Thank you, my lord, for that. I have no difficulty with respect to that portion of the edited note reading now, 'How about right across the street from the hospital. Hey, that was the same bat that was used on Misty and Tanya.' That can go in."

With the winning of this particular issue, Sean Madigan had gained the ability to cross-examine Driver on a very critical issue: the baseball bat. Driver, claiming that he was not the person who had attacked the girls with a baseball bat, could now be asked about his previous knowledge of the bat. In the letter he had written, 'Hey, that was the same bat that was used on Misty and Tanya,' referring to the bat that had been used ninety days earlier in the attack on a woman across from MSA Hospital. In what seemed like an ironic contrast the details of the attack on the other woman were excluded from evidence in the trial.

CROSS-EXAMINATION BEGINS

At first glance Sean Madigan could pass for anyone's grandfather. Slight of build with thinning gray hair and spectacles, he was not the image one might expect for an aggressive Crown prosecutor. Incongruent to this persona, as Madigan began his cross-examination of Terry Driver, it was evident that he was entirely capable of being as aggressive as the situation would require. Commencing the questioning, his tone was cutting and impatient; his questions were short and deliberate. He was on the attack, and Driver, who, up to that point had found a comfortable pace in his testimony, would now find himself confronted with the contradictions in his version of the events.

Madigan:"Summing up your evidence, Mr. Driver, you are telling the court that you are, number one, a rapist, is that right?"

Driver: "I believe so."

Madigan: "A biter of the breast of a dying girl?"

Driver: "Yes."

Madigan: "A sixteen-year-old dying girl?"

Driver: "At the time, I didn't know what age she was."

Madigan: "And how did she look to you?"

Driver: "I beg your pardon?"

Madigan: "How old did she look to you? You saw her naked, didn't you?"

Driver: "Yes, I did."

Madigan: "Well, how did she look to you?"

Driver: "Like a naked woman."

Madigan: "I see. She could have been one year old to one hundred years old, could she?"

Driver: "No, I would probably have thought she was about eighteen, nineteen."

Madigan: "You never sought any medical attention for her?"

Driver: "At the time?"

Madigan: "At any time?"

Driver: "That was my intention."

Madigan: "All right. I'll ask you again. You never sought medical attention for her?"

Driver: "No, I did not."

Madigan: "You yourself have no medical training?"

Driver: "That is correct."

Madigan: "And yet you conveyed her body to the Vedder River and threw her into the water?"

Driver: "Yes."

Madigan: "If she were alive, Mr. Driver, what would you expect would have happened?"

Driver: "I would have got her the same medical—I would

have taken her the same place I would have taken Misty, or I would have made that anonymous phone call."

Madigan: "What does water do to people when they're thrown in unconscious, Mr. Driver?"

Driver: "They would drown."

Madigan: "They would die, wouldn't they?"

Driver: "I guess they would."

Madigan: "And you threw a girl in who was unconscious and she died, didn't she, Mr. Driver?"

Driver: "To me, she had died already."

Madigan: "How do you know?"

Driver: "In my panicked state, that's what I assumed."

Madigan: "Oh, your panicked state. What was the panic, Mr. Driver?"

Driver: "That I thought someone had just died in front of me."

Madigan: "So who cares what you think. You're not medically trained, are you?"

Driver: "That's correct."

Madigan: "You're right on the grounds of the hospital, Mr. Driver, aren't you?"

Driver: "I'm a way from it, yes."

Madigan: "Isn't it the extended care unit that you were on?"

Driver: "At the time, I did not know what it was."

Madigan: "Well, MSA Hospital is next to it?"

Driver: "Yes, but at the time I did not know what that building was."

Madigan: "Well, you knew where the hospital was, didn't you?

Driver: "Yes."

Madigan: "How long would it have taken you to bring her to the hospital?"

Driver: "A few minutes, I guess."

Madigan: "So why didn't you do it?"

Driver: "Because, as I said, I didn't want to get involved with it after what I had seen."

Madigan: "You wanted to play God, didn't you?"

Driver: "I don't understand the meaning because I do not believe in God."

Madigan: "Oh, I see. Yes. You made a medical decision that she was dead, didn't you?"

Driver: "I would assume, yes."

Madigan: "You have no medical training whatsoever?"

Driver: "As a medical professional, no, I do not."

Madigan: "You're not equipped nor educated to make that decision, are you?"

Driver: "No, I am not."

Madigan: "And yet you drove from this hospital grounds to the Vedder River, which is how long away, Mr. Driver?"

Driver: "Probably about twenty minutes."

Madigan: "You drove twenty minutes with her body in your car and chucked her into the water, didn't you?"

Driver: "Yes."

Madigan: "And once you threw her in the water, Mr. Driver, she had no hope whatsoever, did she?'

Driver: "As stated, I thought she was dead."

Madigan: "You don't like answering that one, do you?"

Driver: "I though she had already died."

Madigan: "You're a fisherman, aren't you?"

Driver: "Yes."

Madigan: "And you wade in water, don't you?"

Driver: "Of course."

Madigan: "And you know you'll drown in water if you go into it, don't you?"

Driver: "At the time, I did not think she was alive."

Madigan: "But how do you know? Tell us the procedures you followed to ascertain that she was dead."

Driver: "As I have stated before, as I was engaging in having sex with her and before that, she was making a real raspy-sound breathing. She had—after I had finished, she went into a seizure, and that noise—that breathing that I noticed, that I heard, ceased to exist. I panicked. I believed that I had just finished watching her die and my mind just took itself over. I got scared. I panicked."

Madigan: "What efforts did you make to find out if she was dead?"

Driver: "None."

Madigan: "Yes, absolutely none, isn't that right?"

Driver: "That's correct."

Madigan: "And yet within twenty minutes you threw her into a watery grave, didn't you?

Driver: "I threw her in water."

Madigan: "And that was her grave, wasn't it?"

Driver: "Now, yes, it was."

Madigan: "And yet, according to you, you were over by the doors of the Emergency with Misty Cockerill?"

Driver: "That's correct."

Madigan: "Then why didn't you put Tanya Smith right next to Misty Cockerill?"

Driver: "Because I assumed she had died. I am now dealing with a person that is dead. My semen, maybe hair or something else might be on her. I didn't want anything to be related—related back to me in this manner. I did not want to be connected to a dead person."

Madigan: "But you just told us, Mr. Driver, that you panicked?"

Driver: "That's correct."

Madigan: "And in your panicked state you were able to think about semen, hair, connections to dead people, were you?"

Driver: "That's correct."

Madigan: "You think very clearly when you're panic-stricken, don't you?"

Driver: "I would not say that that would be a clear thought, no."

Madigan: "Did you even think of DNA as you were at it?"

Driver: "No, I did not."

Madigan: "I see. So what you were doing, Mr. Driver, is you were making sure there was no evidence around of your connection to this case, isn't that right?"

Driver: "That's correct."

Madigan: "And after you had done all of this, you say you attended her funeral?"

Driver: "That's correct."

Madigan: "And amazingly, you said your attending her funeral was your way of saying, 'I'm sorry'?"

Driver: "Yes."

Madigan: "Do you actually mean that?"

Driver: "Yes, I do."

Madigan: "Can you tell us anywhere in the evidence you gave for the last few days where you indicated your sorrow?"

Driver: "I do not understand what you are saying."

Madigan: "We—is there anything that you did between October thirteenth and May of 1996, where your sorrow at the death of Tanya Smith was shown to all concerned?"

Driver: "I believe there may have been."

Madigan: "Well, just tell us. Don't keep it from us."

Driver: "I cannot answer that question."

Madigan: "I see. But then you stole her headstone, robbed it off the grave with a crowbar. Does that indicate sorrow, Mr. Driver?"

Driver: "In my mind, yes, it did, because I intended on placing it at the site where she had died."

Madigan: "I see, and that little phrase of yours that you scratched on the headstone, 'Yummy T**,' does that indicate true contrition and sorrow, Mr. Driver?"

Driver: "It was words at the time that popped into my head to use to show at the time that it was me that moved the headstone."

Madigan: "And you threatenedMisty Cockerill, didn't you, Mr. Driver?"

Driver: "I believe that might have been something on there, yes."

Madigan: "Why do you do that, Mr. Driver?

Driver: "Living up to the way the media was sensational-izing all this hype about the Abbotsford Killer."

Madigan: "What business of yours was it what the media were doing, Mr. Driver?"

Driver: "Because I was feeding off of the information."

Madigan: "What do you mean by feeding off of?"

Driver: "The indirect attention."

Madigan: "Oh, yes. You liked the attention, didn't you?"

Driver: "Yes, I would say."

Madigan: "And as your counsel termed them, those taunting phone calls were part of it, weren't they?"

Driver: "Actually, there were two non-taunting phone calls."

Madigan: "Oh, there were two non-taunting ones, but the rest were taunting, weren't they?"

Driver: "I would say that taunting would be a word that would be used too strongly."

Madigan: "Well, your own lawyer called them taunting, so I'm just imitating him."

Driver: "That's—that's fine, that's correct."

Madigan: "What about gloating phone calls?"

Driver: "As what do you mean?"

Madigan: "You were gloating on the phone, 'You can't catch me,' I bit her t**, I'm the Abby Killer.' Aren't they gloating?—"

Mr. Orris interjects: "Well, actually—I'm sorry. He may be paraphrasing what is said, but that's not what was said, so he's putting words attributed to Mr. Driver that are not words that he used. I know the context of his question and that's not the words he used."

Justice Oppal provided direction: "Yes, I appreciate that you're in cross-examination and you're allowed the widest latitude in cross-examination, but if you're going to put words to him, maybe you should put the words that he said."

Madigan: "Well, didn't you say you bit her breast?"

Driver: "Yes, I did."

Madigan: "Didn't you say you were not going to be caught?"

Driver: "I believe so."

Madigan: "Didn't you say, 'Yummy t**'?"

Driver: "At which time?"

Madigan: "On the headstone."

Driver: "I did."

Madigan: "We'll have you look at the headstone to make sure you remember it."

Driver: "I guess I did."

Madigan: "And what about the call on November thirty-first, do you remember what you said there?"

Orris: "Sorry, I think it's October thirty-first."

Madigan: "October thirty-first. Your counsel remembers it."

Orris: "No, he just knows there are not thirty-one days in November."

Madigan: "Good. Do you remember that one?"

Driver: "No, as a matter of fact, I do not remember what I said on that other than when I read it on the transcript itself."

Madigan: "Well, they give you time to listen to it, but one little bit was, 'Eat her f***** c***.' Is the c*** a clitoris, a female organ, is it?"

Driver: "I believe it is."

Madigan: "Yes. Now, why did you say that?"

Driver: "I do not know."

Madigan: "Well, either you said it or you didn't say it?"

Driver: "I said it. I do not know."

Madigan: "You do not know why you said it?"

Driver: "That is correct."

Madigan: "I see. You said it for what, fun?"

Driver: "I said it as the first thing that came into my mind and that was it."

Madigan: "But in relation to a person whose funeral you had attended to show your sorrow, isn't that a most peculiar thing to come into your mind about her?"

Driver: "No, because I was not talking about her."

Madigan: "Who were you talking about?"

Driver: "I would not have a clue."

Madigan: "Wording says, 'Tonight I'm not going to bite her right nipple.' Isn't that Tanya Smith?"

Driver: "If you're referring to being tonight, how could it be? As I said, I do not know why I said what I said there."

Madigan: "Oh, I see. Then why did you phone?"

Driver: "Honestly, I cannot answer that question either."

Madigan: "Now, you have Tourette's?"

Driver: "That is correct."

Madigan: "Is this anything—this Tourette's, is it anything to do with this case?"

Driver: "I do not know how to answer that question."

Madigan: "Well, you're the person?"

Driver: "That is correct."

Madigan: "You're the man who had been walking around Abbotsford for what, five years?"

Driver: "Four years."

Madigan: "Four years? In Vancouver for how many, eight before that?"

Driver: "Longer."

Madigan: "And you're working as a printer?'

Driver: "That's correct."

Madigan: "Now, the time—the last five years, five years prior to 1995, did your Tourette's affect your ability to earn a living?"

Driver: "I did not know what Tourette's really was until I got into Surrey Pretrial."

Madigan: "Oh, yes, and saw a psychiatrist, no doubt."

Driver: "As far as I knew, Tourette's was just the ticks and that was it."

Madigan: "Yes, but as far as you know, outside of learned medical people who may have told you otherwise, you could earn a living with it?"

Driver: "Of course."

Madigan: "You could get married with it?"

Driver: "Yes."

Madigan: "You had children?"

Driver: "Yes."

Madigan: "You had a house or a condo of some kind?"

Driver: "Yes."

Madigan: "You worked every day?"

Driver: "Yes, I did."

Madigan: "You handled rather complicated printing machines?"

Driver: "That's correct."

Madigan: "Did all the business of printing?"

Driver: "I shared in a portion of it, yes."

Madigan: "And you did color printing, which means you had to use different dyes?"

Driver: "That's correct."

Madigan: "You could do all of those things?"

Driver: "That's correct."

Madigan: "You could fish?"

Driver: "Yes."

Madigan: "Walk in the water for hours on end, I suppose?"

Driver: "That's correct."

Madigan: "And your Tourette's never stopped you from doing any of those things?"

Driver: "They did not stop. They did impede."

Madigan: "You drove a car?"

Driver: "That's correct."

Madigan: "Drove your kids in a car?"

Driver: "That's correct."

Madigan: "Drove your wife in a car?"

Driver: "That's correct."

Madigan: "Never stopped you doing that?"

Driver: "It impeded me, yes, it did."

Madigan: "How?"

Driver: "When I tick, my eyes close. I've swerved across the roads."

Madigan: "That's it?"

Driver: "As on part of it, yes, it is."

Madigan: "It didn't make you make these phone calls, did it?"

Driver: "I cannot answer that medically, no."

Madigan: "I see. Is someone else going to answer it medically for you?"

Driver: "I do not know."

Madigan: "So here we have you, a rapist, a biter of breasts, a person who throws a girl into the river, a defacer of tombstones, a threatener of the surviving girl, who you didn't know, of course, right?"

Driver: "That's correct."

Madigan: "You didn't know Misty?"

Driver: "No, I did not."

Madigan: "And yet, even though you've told his lordship that, other than rape, you did nothing else?"

Driver: "That is incorrect."

Madigan: "Oh."

Driver: "By my own actions I caused the death."

Madigan: "Oh, yes. We know that. At the scene you did nothing else, on Bevan, that's what you say? You didn't hit them with the bat, in other words?"

Driver: "That's correct."

Madigan: "Why did you go on this campaign of phone calls, these gloating or taunting phone calls?"

Driver: "The first two were to inform the police on the missing pieces of the puzzle they needed. The other ones I cannot answer."

Madigan: "Strangely enough, on the morning of the fourteenth you ended up down at the Vedder with your two children?"

Driver: "That's correct."

Madigan: "Why did you go down there?"

Driver: "Because I did not hear that she had been found over the scanner. I was concerned that she had not been found yet."

Madigan: "Well, why didn't you make one of those pay phone calls that you became so skilled at, and phone someone to say, 'Look, there might be a body down there in the Vedder, on Number Three and that—whatever the fishing spot is called. Why didn't you do that?"

Driver: "I don't understand what you're trying to get to."

Madigan: "Well, you dumped her body in the Vedder?"

Driver: "Yes."

Madigan: "You're aware the phone calls can't be traced, isn't that right?"

Driver: "They can be traced."

Madigan: "Pay phones, from pay phones?"

Driver: "They can be traced."

Madigan: "Yes, but you made them?"

Driver: "That's correct."

Madigan: "And you scooted away quickly not to be caught?"

Driver: "Actually, I wouldn't say I scooted away quickly, but I did leave, yes."

Madigan: "Yes. Well, why didn't you make a similar call to somebody, anybody, and say, 'There's a body in the Vedder. You better go look'?"

Driver: "Because I did not know if it was found or not yet."

Madigan: "Well, you would be assisting them in finding it, you see. You would tell them it's in the Vedder?"

Driver: "That's correct, and I probably would have done something like that if I had gone to the river and seen that no one was around."

Madigan: "Why did you phone Cliff?"

Driver: "I do not know."

Madigan: "You phoned more than Cliff, didn't you?"

Driver: "Yes, I did."

Madigan: "Who else did you phone?"

Driver: "At the time, I do not know. I do know that it is 85 Radio Max."

Madigan: "Yeah."

Driver: "I have no recollection of making that phone call whatsoever."

Madigan: "And who else? There are more."

Driver: "You tell me, because I wouldn't know then."

Madigan: "BCTV, didn't you phone them?"

Driver: "I do not know."

Madigan: "What do you mean you don't know?"

Driver: "Exactly what I'm saying. I do not recall."

Madigan: "You just forgot, have you?"

Driver: "I believe so."

Madigan: "I see. Well, why did you phone Radio Max?"

Driver: "I do not know. I do not remember making that phone call."

Madigan: "I see. You just went right out of your head, did it?"

Driver: "That's right."

Madigan: "Now, Cliff is a good friend of yours, isn't he?"

Driver: "Yes."

Madigan: "You're telling the court that when you phoned, you had just been caught up in a very unfortunate business, isn't that right?"

Driver: "In what sense?"

Madigan: "Well, you had been at the extended care parking lot and seen two girls unconscious, had raped one, and then carted her off and chucked her in the Vedder. All that had occurred before you phoned Cliff?"

Driver: "Yes."

Madigan: "Plus, you believed at that time that you didn't want to connect yourself with this event because it might get you into trouble?"

Driver: "That's correct."

Madigan: "Why didn't you tell him, 'Cliff, I don't want to phone them because I'll get in trouble. Would you phone for me?'"

Driver: "I don't understand what you are trying to get at."

Madigan: "Why didn't you ask Cliff for help?"

Driver: "For help for what?"

Madigan: "To get you out of this fix you found yourself in. You were in a fix?"

Driver: "Yes, I was."

Madigan: "I thought this whole case is about you helping the police, mind you in a funny way, but—"

Driver: "I don't see what getting him involved would make any difference."

Madigan: "Well, you'd solved the whole thing. There would be no Abby Killer, it would be solved, and the real killer would be pursued, wouldn't he?"

Driver: "I don't see what you are trying to get to, so I can't answer."

Madigan: "I see. Why didn't you call your brother?"

Driver: "I still don't understand what you're trying to get to."

Madigan: "Did you need help on the morning of the fourteenth of October, 1995, when you were out at the Vedder River?"

Driver: "Help in what way?"

Madigan: "To solve the crime you had seemingly stumbled upon the night before?"

Driver: "I'd have no answer to that."

Madigan: "Solving that crime was of no interest to you?"

Driver: "As I said, I don't know what you're trying to say, so I can't answer the question you're asking."

Madigan: "I see. And you testified here that after certain events you eventually found yourself on this grassy knoll, as you've called it, in the corner of the parking lot, and there you saw two young girls lying unconscious on the ground?"

Driver: "Yes."

Madigan: "Were they drunk?"

Driver: "I don't know."

Madigan: "How were they lying unconscious on the ground, do you know?"

Driver: "Because I assume after seeing the bat on the ground that they were beaten."

Madigan: "And didn't you mention that you saw blood on the nose of Tanya Smith?"

Driver: "Yes."

Madigan: "Now, how did you think they got there?"

Driver: "I didn't."

Madigan: "I thought you told us—I thought you said that you did think about it?"

Driver: "No, you just asked me how I thought they got there. I do not know how they got there."

Madigan: "I see. Well, what did you think they were doing there, other than lying on the ground?"

Driver: "That they were assaulted."

Madigan: "Yes, we got there. Yes, they were assaulted, and the assaults were of such severity that they were unconscious on the ground?"

Driver: "Yes."

Madigan: "And you also got the bat involved in the assault, didn't you?"

Driver: "In what manner?"

Madigan: "That someone had hit them with the bat and that's why they were lying unconscious on the ground?"

Driver: "Yes."

Madigan: "Now, that, according to you anyway, is what you knew?"

Driver: "Yes."

Madigan: "Somebody had beaten these girls with a bat?"

Driver: "That's correct."

Madigan: "And according to you, despite your lack of medical knowledge, one of them had been killed?"

Driver: "That's correct."

Madigan: "You're age what, thirty-two?"

Driver: "Yes."

Madigan: "You realize what murder is?"

Driver: "Yes, I do."

Madigan: "So you had been a witness to a murder, hadn't you?"

Driver: "Yes."

Madigan: "Well, didn't you want to solve it?"

Driver: "No."

Madigan: "Didn't you want to get yourself out of the murder and put yourself in the right position of a rapist?"

Driver: "No, that is not what was going through my mind."

Madigan: "What was going through your mind?"

Driver: "What was going through my mind, a piece that I do remember, was that because I have not gotten her medical treatment, I have sexually assaulted her, she has died.

I know the way the police work. I would still be held as a prime suspect."

Madigan: "But if they didn't know who you were, how could you be held as a prime suspect?"

Driver: "You're asking me to get involved with it."

Madigan: "Yes."

Driver: "That's the reason why."

Madigan: "Well, why didn't you ask Cliff to do it for you?"

Driver: "I was by myself."

Madigan: "You had a phone. You actually talked to Cliff?"

Driver: "That's right, yes."

Madigan: "Why didn't you say, 'Cliff, I want to see you. I've got a real problem.' You didn't do that, did you?"

Driver: "Of course not."

Madigan: "You just said, 'I'm down here with my kids and I'm looking at a crime scene'?"

Driver: "I believe so, yes."

Madigan: "And what did you tell the Radio Max fellow, the same thing? 'I'm down here.'"

Driver: "I don't know."

Madigan: "I'm looking at a crime scene."

Driver: "I do not know."

Madigan: "Well, you wouldn't be singing to him, would you? You'd be telling him about the scene you were at, wouldn't you?"

Driver: "I do not recall."

Madigan: "I see. What about other members of your family, why didn't you phone them?"

Driver: "Why would I?"

Madigan: "Because of the fix you were in?"

Driver: "Why would I?"

Madigan: "Now, isn't it true that in 1996, members of your family said, 'Terry, we heard broadcasts of a voice and we're sad to tell you it sounds like you,' didn't they?"

Driver: "I don't recall word for word, no."

Madigan: "But in effect, that's what they told you."

Driver: "Yes."

Madigan: "And they said, 'You should clear it up, Terry,' didn't they?"

Driver: "Yes."

Madigan: "And you should give whatever samples these policemen want to clear your name off."

Driver: "Yes."

Madigan: "Isn't that right?"

Driver: "Yes."

Madigan: "And you went to a lawyer?"

Driver: "Yes."

Madigan: "Right, Harris?"

Driver: "That's correct."

Madigan: "On the fourteenth. Why didn't you phone up Harris or similar lawyer?"

Driver: "Pardon me?"

Madigan: "Why didn't you phone a lawyer on the fourteenth and say, 'Have I got bad news for you'?"

Driver: "I can't answer that question. I do not know."

Madigan: "Because you had beaten those girls with the bat, hadn't you?"

Driver: "No, I had not."

Madigan: "Well, why did you have it then?"

Driver: "Have what?"

Madigan: "The bat?"

Driver: "Because it was lying on the ground beside her."

Madigan: "Oh, yes. What about the note you'd flung thought the window of the house?"

Driver: "Yes."

Madigan: "The one where you said you were looking for publicity or something, you said?"

Driver: "That's correct."

Madigan: "Didn't you claim the bat there?"

Driver: "Yes, I did."

Madigan: "All right. And why did you hit them with the bat?"

Driver: "The note was made in February. The assault took place in October, and the other one, I believe, what you're talking about, took place in August or September. I knew about the bat that was there because it was at the scene of the October incident."

Madigan: "Why did you claim possession of the bat that beat Tanya and Misty?"

Driver: "Because it was the bat that was at the scene of the attack."

Madigan: "How do you know? Is there someone's name on it or something?"

Driver: "Because I saw it there."

Madigan: "A bat was there?"

Driver: "That is correct."

Madigan: "How did you know it was the same bat that you had earlier on? How did you know?"

Driver: "In what text are you talking about? Do you mean out of the letter?"

Madigan: "You made the letter up. I didn't."

Driver: "Because the letter was made up in February."

Madigan: "Yes, by you."

Driver: "That's right."

Madigan: "On your computer?"

Driver: "That's right."

Madigan: "Typed by you?"

Driver: "That's right."

Madigan: "Printed by you?"

Driver: "That's right."

Madigan: "And flung through the window by you?"

Driver: "That's correct."

Madigan: "Now, what does it mean?"

Driver: "It means that I'm trying to make it look like this person is bad."

Madigan: "Oh, that's true. How about the phrase, 'How about right across the street from the hospital? That was the same bat that was used on Misty and Tanya'?"

Driver: "Yes."

Madigan: "Why did you type that?"

Driver: "As I explained already, I knew about the bat being at the incident in October."

Madigan: "The one you'd chucked into the dyke?"

Driver: "In the ditch."

Madigan: "Yes."

Driver: "Yes."

Madigan: "It's the same bat. The same bat to what? You typed this?"

Driver: "That's correct."

Madigan: "And what did you mean when you typed it?"

Driver: "I do not know. The words just came out of my head at the moment I was typing it."

Madigan: "Oh, I see. You just chattered along on the keys, did you?"

Driver: "Basically."

Madigan: "And when you proofread it at the end, you said, 'Aw, who cares?'"

Driver: "I didn't even proofread it."

Madigan: "I see. Why did you write on Misty's photo, 'Lucky to be Alive'?"

Driver: "I do not know. I do not even recall writing it."

Madigan: "But you did?"

Driver: "Yes, I must have."

Madigan: "Why did you steal the headstone from her grave?"

Driver: "I believe I've already told you the reason why."

Madigan: "Well, tell me again. I like hearing it."

Driver: "Because I wanted to—I believe that the head-stone belonged at the place that she had died."

Madigan: "I see. Now, this is long after the event, well, months after the event?"

Driver: "Yes."

Madigan: "And you also claimed in your evidence that when you found out that she had in fact been drown, you said you were in shock, like someone had punched him in the stomach or ripped his guts out?"

Driver: "Yes."

Madigan: "Now, that kind of guy I'm talking about, why would you use all these insulting terms when that was your condition?"

Driver: "I honestly can't answer why, what was going through my head."

Madigan: "Because insulting terms they were, isn't that correct?"

Driver: "That's correct."

Madigan: "They were grossly insulting?"

Driver: "Yes."

Madigan: "And if someone had said that about your wife in your presence, you'd have attacked them, wouldn't you?"

Driver: "No, I would not have."

Madigan: "You wouldn't like it?"

Driver: "I would not like it, yes."

Madigan: "Now, why were you trying to solve something using those terms?"

Driver: "Honestly, I can't say. The only thing I know what was happening also at the time is I was feeding off of the media coverage and the sensationalism."

Madigan: "You're blaming the media for all of this, are you?"

Driver: "No."

Madigan: "Were the media people up at Bevan Street when these unfortunate kids were lying dying on the ground?"

Driver: "No."

Madigan: "Were they there when you had sex with Tanya Smith?"

Driver: "No."

Madigan: "Where they there when you bit her breast?"

Driver: "No."

Madigan: "Were they there when you chucked her into the Vedder?"

Driver: "No."

Madigan: "Were they there when you stole her tombstone?"

Driver: "No."

Madigan: "Were they there when you defaced it?"

Driver: "No."

Madigan: "Well, why do you blame the media?"

Driver: "I was feeding off—"

Mr. Orris intervenes: "I don't—excuse me. I think he said specifically he did not blame the media. That was his evidence."

Justice Oppal: "Yes, he said, 'I was feeding off the media coverage,' and you asked him if he blamed the media and he said, 'No.'"

Madigan: "Well, are you blaming the media or not?"

Driver: "No, I am not."

Madigan: "What do you mean by 'feeding off the coverage'?"

Driver: "Off the sensationalism."

Madigan: "You're blaming yourself?"

Driver: "In what manner."

Madigan: "Well, using all these words?"

Driver: "It's what the media thrives for."

Madigan: "What about yourself, thriving on it?"

Driver: "In what sense, in the attention it was receiving?"

Madigan: "Yes."

Driver: "Yes, I would have to answer."

Madigan: "Now, why would you do that? Why would you be feeding off of this matter after such a shocking event of the 14 of October, 1995?"

Driver: "I don't know."

Madigan: "You playing a game with everyone in Abbotsford, were you?"

Driver: "No, that was not the intention."

Madigan: "Was this a game of cat and mouse?"

Driver: "It might have been to a degree, yes."

Madigan: "Now, why would you engage in such a game if you were innocent of any killing of a person on Bevan Street?"

Driver: "I was not innocent."

Madigan: "No, but that was on the Vedder. I'm talking about Bevan Street."

Driver: "Okay. Can you rephrase it then, please?"

Madigan: "All right. Why would you act in such a fashion if you had nothing to do with the beating death, in fact, of one girl and the serious injury to another girl on Bevan Street?"

Driver: "I don't know if I can answer that, because I don't know what you're trying to say there."

Madigan: "So you had nothing to do with the beating of those girls?"

Driver: "That is correct."

Madigan: "That all you did was have sex and bite her breast with one of them?"

Driver: "Yes."

Madigan: "And convey the other to the hospital, at least the parking lot?"

Driver: "Yes."

Madigan: "Now, why would you be glorying in being called the Abbotsford Killer?"

Driver: "That's just a name the media made up."

Madigan: "Yes, but they made it up for the killer of Tanya Smith, didn't they?"

Driver: "No, they made it up to the—if I believe right—for the phone calls and stuff like that had happened afterwards."

Madigan: "But they were talking about the killer of Tanya Smith?"

Driver: "Yes."

Madigan: "Now, why would you take that tag and wear it so proudly?"

Driver: "I wouldn't say I was wearing it proudly, no."

Madigan: "Then why were you making these phone calls?"

Driver: "I cannot answer that question. I do not know."

Madigan: "But you were there and I wasn't?"

Driver: "That's right."

Madigan: "Why did you make the phone calls?"

Driver: "I do not know."

Madigan: "Why were you gloating in the phone calls?"

Driver: "I do not know."

Madigan: "Why did you steal the headstone?"

Driver: "As I said before, because I believed that it belonged in the spot where she had died."

Madigan: "Well, surely to goodness the wishes of the parents had something to do with this, didn't it?"

Driver: "I was not thinking at the time."

Madigan: "Well, of course you were thinking. You went there, didn't you?"

Driver: "Yes."

Madigan: "You got a crowbar out and yanked it off?"

Driver: "I was not thinking about other people's thoughts."

Madigan: "You mean you regularly go to graveyards and yank off headstones, do you?"

Driver: "No, that was the first time I ever did that."

Madigan: "Why did you do it?"

Driver: "Because I believed that it needed to be over where she actually died."

Madigan: "Despite the wishes of her parents?"

Driver: "I did not know her parents. I did not know what the wishes would be."

Madigan: "Now, why do you think they put a gravestone on their daughter's grave?"

Driver: "Why else would you? That's where your daughter's buried."

Madigan: "Did you read it?"

Driver: "I believe so."

Madigan: "What did it say?"

Driver: "I do not remember."

With this question answered, Justice Oppal intervened and called for the afternoon adjournment. This ended the first morning of cross-examination. The complete cross-examination would last two full court days and extend into the morning of the third day.

During the remaining cross-examination, the questions and the explanations would fall into a similar pattern. Driver would excuse away motivation for his actions by saying that he was feeding off the media attention and giving the media what they wanted. When cornered on the issue of what he was thinking at the time of a particular incident, he would claim either not to remember what he was thinking at the time or alternately would maintain that the thought had just popped into his head at the time. Madigan doggedly pursued the issues surrounding each event, the attack site, phone calls, the theft of the headstone, and the letter, one after the other. Then he would pursue them again and, on occasion, would illustrate a significant point. Recounting the entire narrative of the remaining cross-examination will not be attempted in this review of the evidence; only the critical points will be illustrated.

During the remaining days of the cross-examination, some of the critical points that were covered included the scanner issue, previous knowledge of the baseball bat, and the extent to which Misty's blood was present in the front of Driver's car.

On the issue of the scanner, Madigan posed the question: "There was nothing wrong with your mind when you were—"

Driver: "I thought of a lot of the things, actually, at the time. I can't recall a lot of the stuff that was going through my head at the time, because of the state that I was in."

Madigan: "What state were you in?"

Driver: "In a very panicked state, scared state."

Madigan: "You mean in your panicked state you still had time to set your radar and your machine to the Chilliwack RCMP?"

Driver: "Yes."

Madigan: "I see. This is how you react when you're in a panicked state, is it?"

Driver: "My mind runs, yes."

Madigan: "I see. And you knew it was the Chilliwack RCMP and not the Abbotsford Police you were going to set these two devices to?"

Driver: "Chilliwack RCMP are who frequent—who patrol the highway."

Madigan: "I see. But you were thinking. You could distinguish between Abbotsford Police and Chilliwack RCMP?"

Driver: "Yes."

Late on the second day of cross-examination, there was a significant exchange in relation to the notation in the letter referring to the baseball bat.

Madigan asked, referring to the letter: "And you prepared this thing?"

Driver: "Yes."

Madigan: "And you put the pliers in there?"

Driver: "Yes."

Madigan: "To give it weight, I guess?"

Driver: "Yes."

Madigan: "And the Abby Killer on the cover?"

Driver: "That's correct."

Madigan: "All yours?"

Driver: "Yes."

Madigan: "Why?"

Driver: "I think I already stated to the fact I'm feeding off of the medial frenzy of this thing. That note in a way was giving them what they wanted. I was intending on the police to release that note to the media."

Madigan: "But this is a murder case you're talking about."

Driver: "Yes."

Madigan: "Well, why were you writing this stuff about murder?"

Driver: "I don't know. I've already said what was on my mind at that time."

Madigan: "Well, what about this little statement down there, 'How about right across the street from the hospital.

Hey, that was the same bat,' and I'll emphasize same bat 'that was used on Misty and Tanya.' And here you're saying that you had that bat before this particular night, aren't you?"

Driver: "Implying, yes."

Madigan: "What did you put it down there for?"

Driver: "Because of one of the incidences that was in that letter."

Madigan: "Well, why were you claiming possession of the bat that you were not claiming in your evidence here?"

Driver: "I don't know if I can even answer that question because if it relates to the matter of the stuff that is not allowed—that does not have to be admitted into the courts."

In this exchange, Driver is acknowledging that he was claiming ownership of the bat but then falls back on the exclusion of evidence to avoid answering the full question.

On the third and final morning of cross-examination, the issue of blood in the front of Driver's car was once again addressed.

Madigan: "Now, you said that you took Misty to the hospital. Was she bleeding when you took her to the hospital?"

Driver: "I can't recall actually."

Madigan: "Now, you've seen all the exhibits here and you've seen her clothing with all the blood on it?"

Driver: "Yes."

Madigan: "Did you notice that?"

Driver: "Not at the time, no."

Madigan: "And she is sitting up in your car in the front seat?"

Driver: "Yeah."

Madigan: "And you know the back of her head was caved in?"

Driver: "She was sitting over to the side towards the door. As I was driving, I was actually holding onto her."

Madigan: "And when you got her out, was your car covered in blood?"

Driver: "There was some blood on the car, yes."

Madigan: "The front seat?"

Driver: "No."

Madigan: "Where?"

Driver: "By the door."

Madigan: "And I guess you cleaned it up when you cleaned out the carpet and all the rest, did you?"

Driver: "Yes."

Madigan: "Because she was bleeding?"

Driver: "At the time I didn't know—I assumed after I was cleaning the car that she had been bleeding, yes."

With this question, Driver contradicted his previous testimony that there was no blood in the front of his car. Shortly after this exchange, Sean Madigan would conclude his cross-examination, and Driver would return to the prisoner dock to once again become an observer of the proceedings.

In this trial, the purpose of cross-examination was to review and challenge the version of events offered by the accused and test the truthfulness of that story. In cross-examination, Madigan asked many probing questions about Driver's version of the events, why he did certain things, and what he was thinking at the time. To some of those observing, it appeared that Driver either could not answer or would not answer many of these questions. There were contradictions of his own previous testimony and what seemed to be convenient lapses of memory. Could the judge possibly find this story believable? Only time would tell.

THE PSYCHOLOGY BEHIND THE DEFENCE

Driver was immediately followed on the stand by his own mother, called by the defence to start building a profile of Driver's medical and behavioral history. Driver's mother told the court that Terry was a "bad child" who would routinely destroy things and rarely responded to discipline. Unmanageable at the age of five years, he needed to be institutionalized to deal with his emotional and behavioral problems. Several years later, Driver's parents would divorce. When he finally left the institution, he would move to live with his father. Driver's mother's testimony set the stage for the introduction of three doctors who would each testify regarding Driver's various afflictions.

Dr. Mort Dorn, a medical doctor and surgeon, was himself a sufferer of Tourette's syndrome and Obsessive Compulsive Disorder (OCD). Dr. Dorn testified that most people who suffer from Tourette's syndrome also experience varying degrees of the associated disorders of OCD and Attention Deficit Hyperactivity Disorder (ADHD).

Dr. Dorn offered that sufferers of OCD sometimes have an inability to control their strong urges.

They lack the ability to delay gratification, and they are always seeking stimulation, almost to the degree of being addicted to turmoil. His own experience with the afflictions included a distain for authority and being impatient with processes as routine as airport security screening.

As he testified, Dr. Dorn's own Tourettes's symptoms were apparent. He would repeatedly go through a ritual of straightening his glasses, tapping the microphone, and pulling on the lapel of his suit. Under cross-examination, Dr. Dorn agreed that he had certainly gained control over his own afflictions to the extent that he was able to perform surgeries and pilot a private aircraft.

Dr. Roy O'Shaughnessy, a forensic psychiatrist, was the next medical expert called for the defence. He had conducted extensive interviews with Driver. He offered to the court that, in outward appearances, Driver's life was very conventional; however, he had a secret life and compulsions. On the surface, he had a conventional life, and one would not expect this man to be involved in criminal behaviors.

In his opinion, Driver was not a very self-aware person. He was disappointed by his rejection from a policing career. He admired his father and had wanted to follow in his footsteps.

He agreed with Dr. Dorn that Driver was suffering from the three disorders of Tourette's syndrome, Obsessive Compulsive Disorder (OCD), and Attention Deficit Hyperactivity Disorder (ADHD). He said that these disorders affected or inhibited Driver's ability to learn social values as a youth, and this left him with strong sexual impulses that he had difficulty controlling. During his interviews with Dr. O'Shaughnessy, Driver disclosed that he would often be involved in some activity and would find it necessary to go into the bathroom or the bushes to disrobe and masturbate.

O'Shaughnessy stated that Driver denied ever having rape fantasies but did say that he had fantasies about having sex with women who were passed-out drunk.

In cross-examination, Madigan asked the doctor if Driver's decision to have sex with an injured, unconscious girl was psychopathic behavior. O'Shaughnessy replied that it was certainly callous; however, he did not believe that Driver was a psychopath.

Dr. Robert Ley was the final expert forensic psychiatrist to testify for the defence. He testified that he had interviewed Driver on six occasions for a total of twenty hours. He had performed IQ tests that showed Driver had an average IQ of ninety-seven. The score was averaged between a low verbal IQ of eighty-eight and an above-average performance IQ of 114. He said that this indicated that Driver performed better in visual and spatial testing. He told the court that Driver was an introverted loner who had experienced significant rejection in his life.

He stated that the afflictions of Obsessive Compulsive Disorder and Attention Deficit Disorder caused Driver to have a rare combination of both compulsiveness and impulsiveness. With this, he supported Dr. O'Shaughnessy's observations that Driver was a highly impulsive person who had an "intense ambivalence" toward authority, which translated into a sort of love-hate relationship with the police. He pointed out that during the time when Driver watched the police from

a distance as they dusted the phone booth for prints, he felt
superior and felt as though he had triumphed over them.

In a challenge to the testimony of impulsive behavior, under cross-examination by Crown Prosecutor Neil
Mackenzie, Dr. Ley admitted that Driver had told him during interviews that when he made his pay phone calls, he
always held the phone with the palm of his hand, thus making sure not to leave his prints. Contrary to his testimony
about only going to the cemetery once on an impulse, Driver
had disclosed to Dr. Ley that he had actually visited the
cemetery on one occasion prior to stealing the headstone.

Collectively, the three doctors had constructed the profile
of a young man with an extremely troubled childhood and an
equally troubled and disturbing adult lifestyle. Much of what
they said in regards to Driver's hunger for attention and need
to feel superior to the police did fit with what had happened.
Would the court believe that the influence of the three afflictions was supportive of Driver's entire version of the events?
Again, we would wait.

As the defence rested their case, Sean Madigan was
given the opportunity to call psychiatrists to present rebuttal
evidence. Madigan elected not to do so, believing that the
expert evidence presented by the three defence doctors was
not strong enough to require rebuttal.

THE TRIAL CONCLUDES

The evidence was all in now. After nineteen days of trial, with sixty-eight witnesses and over one hundred exhibits in evidence, the Crown and defence would move into their summations.

The summations would be relatively short and without surprise, content for anyone who had listened to the trial. On October 7, 1997, summations were presented.

For the defence, Glen Orris would maintain that his client was out scanner chasing and was drawn to the Bevan attack site after seeing an unknown suspect fleeing the area. Here he found the two girls unconscious and, unable to control his sexual urges because of his obsessive afflictions, he had sex with the unconscious Tanya Smith. Believing Smith had died after the sex act, he loaded her body into the trunk of his car and took her to the Vedder River, where he placed her into the water. On the point of intent to commit murder, Orris would argue that Driver believed Smith was already dead, and therefore he did not have the intent to take her life when he placed her body into the river.

Orris pointed to the differences in Misty's descriptions in composites drawings from Driver's appearance and Misty's failure to pick Driver out of the photo lineup as being supportive of the story of an unknown suspect fleeing the scene.

Orris contended that the rest of Driver's post-crime behavior, the phone calls to police, the theft of the headstone, and the letter through the window were all consistent with the afflictions of Tourette's syndrome, Obsessive Compulsive Disorder, and Attention Deficit Hyperactivity Disorder.

The summation of the Crown was equally short and to the point. Sean Madigan would maintain that Driver had made up his version of the events to weave his way around and include all of the points of evidence that could be proven. His story was not designed to deny all involvement, but rather to minimize his responsibility for the death of Tanya Smith and to deny any involvement in the attempted murder of Misty Cockerill. Madigan maintained that Driver's version of the events lacked credibility and should not be accepted by the court. His communications with the police in phone calls and written messages on the headstone and letter were true confessions to the murder of Tanya Smith and the attempted murder of Misty Cockerill.

THE VERDICT

On Thursday, October 16, 1997, in the New Westminster Supreme Courtroom, where Justice Oppal would hand down his verdict, was filled to capacity. It had been nine days since the Crown and defence submitted their summations. Notably, it was exactly two years and two days from the day that Misty and Tanya were attacked on the back parking lot of the MSA Extended Care Unit. The families of both the victims and the accused had been waiting with anxious anticipation to hear the outcome.

For Driver's brother and mother, who believed Terry's version of the events, there were probably hopes that a verdict of second-degree murder would be the outcome.

In contrast, for the victim and victim families, they were aware that anything less than a verdict of first degree would lead to an appeal. The prospect of having to go through another trial was unthinkable.

When Justice Oppal began his presentation of the verdict, there was a strained silence in the courtroom. Everyone listened intensely to every word, waiting for the first hint or indication of which direction the court would rule.

In the traditional format that judges follow in a verdict delivery, Justice Oppal provided a verbal outline of what he had heard and the legal arguments he had considered.

When he finally reached the point where he would reveal his decision, the pent-up emotion in the courtroom was almost unbearable. Finally, Justice Oppal spoke those words of relief: "In summary, I am satisfied, beyond a reasonable doubt, that the accused is guilty as charged on count one." Count one was the murder of Tanya Smith, followed by a similar ruling of guilty for the attempted murder of Misty Cockerill.

As these words were uttered by the judge, a tidal wave of emotion swept through the courtroom. The victim families cried and held each other, finally released by the conclusion of this ordeal in justice. The family of the accused sat in quiet acceptance.

These were not the only words that Justice Oppal would have for Terry Driver. He would tell Driver, "I simply cannot find the words to describe and depict your horrible crimes. It seems to me you jeopardized the safety and security of a whole town. You attacked two women who were enjoying life. They were on their way to a birthday party. What could be safer than that? They did nothing to you. You murdered Tanya Smith for your own sexual gratification. I cannot understand the motivation for these vicious and senseless attacks on these two innocent people. There is simply no excuse for what you have done."

He went on to tell Driver, "I watched you during your testimony and saw not one degree of remorse. You weren't content to just murder a person, if I can put it that way. You taunted the police, and in an ultimate act of insensitivity to the family, you stole the gravestone."

In articulating the reasons for his ruling, Justice Oppal commented, "I must say that the accused was not a satisfactory witness. There were significant inconsistencies in both his conduct and his testimony."

Oppal then outlined the reasons for his finding. They included:

- Driver's claim that he did not want to use his cell phone to call police because it could be traced was inconsistent with the fact that he had already used the cell phone that same night to call police and report that bike theft.

- Justice Oppal did not believe Driver's claim that he had driven Misty to the front of the hospital. He pointed out that the doctors and nurses all testified that Misty was covered in blood, yet Driver claimed that there was no blood on the front seat of his car. This was inconsistent with other evidence before the court.

- Justice Oppal also felt that Driver's story of panicking after Tanya had apparently died in front of him was contradicted by the fact that he apparently had the presence of mind to adjust his police scanner to the RCMP Channel and set his radar detector as he was driving with Tanya's body to the Vedder River.

- The baseball bat also became an issue for comment. In the judge's opinion, if Driver was not the person who attacked the two girls, there would be no reason for him to take the bat from the crime scene. He offered the court no reasonable explanation for taking the bat.

- Although he felt that the medical evidence did provide

some insight into Driver's behavior, Justice Oppal
did not believe that the three afflictions of Tourette's
syndrome, Obsessive Compulsive Disorder, and
Attention Deficit Hyperactivity Disorder provided
Driver with any excuse for his acts.

• Driver's testimony of making phone calls to help
police with the missing pieces of the puzzle was
not believable. If that was his motive, he had
clearly left out any mention of the man he saw
leaving the scene, which was "arguably the most
important piece of the puzzle."

In response to differences in Misty's description of the
attacker and failure to identify Driver in the photo lineup,
Justice Oppal said, "One could hardly expect her to recall
with accuracy and precision the circumstances of the incident." He went on to point out, "Composite drawings have
serious limitations and, as result, are of limited value."

At the conclusion of articulating his verdict, Justice Oppal
sentenced Terry Driver to life in prison without possibility of
parole for twenty-five years for the murder of Tanya Smith and
ten years to be served concurrently for the attempted murder of
Misty Cockerill. In handing down this sentence, Oppal stated,
"Life means life," signifying the gravity of the outcome.

At the conclusion of his verdict, Justice Oppal turned to
Driver in the prisoner dock and asked if he had anything
to say. Driver, showing no emotion, spoke with a clear and
unaffected voice, "No," and with that, the trial concluded.

As we all left the courtroom that day, the news media were
swarming about gathering facts and observations as they emerged.
Misty and the Smith family members paused to express their

thanks to the prosecutors and the police. It was finally over, and people could try to start getting on with their lives.

A final press conference was held at the Abbotsford Police Office. Misty Cockerill and her family, along with the family of Tanya Smith, sat before a sea of microphones and provided their comments on the conclusion of the case and the conviction of Terry Driver. For the justice system, police, and prosecution, the outcome of the investigation and trial were a success. Gail and Terry Smith correctly reframed everyone's perspective when they pointed out that, no matter what the outcome was, their daughter, Tanya, was still gone from them forever. For the Smiths, as it is for many victims and victim families, the outcome of the justice system process only serves as an empty anti-climax to the painful realities of a crime thrust upon them.

EPILOGUE

After the final press conference held at the Abbotsford Police Office, the media frenzy that had become routine during the seven-month investigation and again throughout the trial finally diminished. There were some short revivals of interest as Driver was convicted of two assaults on Abbotsford women that he described in his letter. With these convictions he received a Dangerous Offender designation. This designation should have some effect on Driver's eligibility for parole when it becomes available under the "faint hope" clause in the year 2011. In 2021, Driver will have served twenty-five years of his life and will be eligible for parole. He will be fifty-seven years of age.

Shortly after the conviction in 1997, Driver's brother and mother asked to be paid the reward that had been offered for information leading to the arrest and conviction of the killer. The brother maintained that the family still believes Terry's version of the story. He wanted to collect the reward to conduct research into Tourette's syndrome. Payment of the reward was deferred until all appeals had been heard. Finally, in December of 2003, with all avenues of appeal exhausted, Driver's mother and brother were awarded ten thousand dollars.

For the Abbotsford Police Department and other police agencies that partnered to form the Homicide Task Force, this case represents a proud success story of interagency cooperation and resource sharing. In the careers of the officers from those many police agencies, the investigation is something they will never forget. As the Team Commander, I will never forget the amazing dedication of our team. Many of them put their personal lives on hold for those seven months and gave their entire attention to capturing the killer. Several team members, including Bill Emery and Kevin MacLeod, moved on to take lead roles in the Provincial Integrated Homicide Investigation (IHIT) Teams. The IHIT teams are now full-time multi-agency homicide investigation teams that concentrate on major homicide cases throughout British Columbia.

Misty Cockerill recovered from her injuries. The end of the case allowed her to return to a normal life. It allowed for her family to put aside the stress of the ordeal and resume their lives as well. The Abbotsford Police presented Misty with a special plaque honoring her courage and resolve throughout the investigation and the trial.

Called upon as a speaker for violence against women, Misty presents an inspirational survival story as a victim of violence. Misty, at the time of this writing, is now a young mother. She volunteers part-time as a victim support worker for the Abbotsford Police Victim Services Section.

In Abbotsford and neighboring Fraser Valley communities, the conviction of Terry Driver signaled the end of a horrific fearful chapter in our history. The frightening implicit message behind these events is: a killer of this magnitude could surface in any community, and a very normal-looking neighbor could turn out to be a devious murderer. It is unclear if the residual fear from this event will ever go away completely, and perhaps it shouldn't.

Even though predators who commit such horrible crimes are rare, it is important to remember that they do exist. Knowing they exist can have one of two outcomes. It can cause the fear that will make us all victims, or it can empower us to recognize these killers as a remote risk and prepare us to deal with them swiftly when they impose themselves on the safety of our communities.

A Police Officer's Prayer

I swore to serve and to protect
Spoke from my heart with pride
And now I pray that every day
This oath I can abide

Lord, grant me instincts and the skills
To stop those who cause harm
Give me courage if called to fight
To be the law's strong arm

Keep compassion in my heart
For all those whom we serve
Let me not forget the powers I use
Take wisdom to preserve

Temptations that will cross my path
Must never make me stray
Living honor, truth, and wisdom
For these great strengths I pray

For comrades who have sworn to serve
Backup is our trust reserved
Let no threat deter me from their side
Help me be what they deserve

If on duty I should die
Lord, accept me to your house
Give comfort to my children
Strength and courage to my spouse

listen|imagine|view|experience

AUDIO BOOK DOWNLOAD INCLUDED WITH THIS BOOK!

In your hands you hold a complete digital entertainment package. Besides purchasing the paper version of this book, this book includes a free download of the audio version of this book. Simply use the code listed below when visiting our website. Once downloaded to your computer, you can listen to the book through your computer's speakers, burn it to an audio CD or save the file to your portable music device (such as Apple's popular iPod) and listen on the go!

How to get your free audio book digital download:

1. Visit www.tatepublishing.com and click on the e|LIVE logo on the home page.
2. Enter the following coupon code:
   9093-4b4b-e125-46c9-aa8e-386e-2821-7d41
3. Download the audio book from your e|LIVE digital locker and begin enjoying your new digital entertainment package today!